For
Bernice
Goo Goo

Radiant
Light
Always,
Nona

Chopstick Childhood

In a Town of Silver Spoons

Orphaned at the Ming Quong Home,
Los Gatos, CA

Nona Mock Wyman

Original Cover design by Wendy K. Lee
Original Chinese calligraphy by Les Ong

Copyright © 1997-2018 by Nona Mock Wyman, with additional material added in 1999. 2nd Edition 2018, book redesign and format by Susan Settle with editing by Conrad Houghtby, Taylor Callan and Donna Van Sant.

For permission requests, write to the publisher, addressed "Attention: Permissions Coordinator," at the address below.
dvs Publishing
2824 Winthrop Ave.
San Ramon, CA 94583

ISBN: 978-0-9977484-1-3

Printed in the United States of America

*This book is dedicated to all the
Ming Quong girls and teachers
whose lives intertwined with mine...*

Author's Notes

In 1992, while working at my store in Walnut Creek, I met a New York poet, Sue Tkach. She was in California for a haiku (poem) conference. I had never heard of haiku, so she explained that it was an ancient form of Japanese poetry, consisting of seventeen syllables, divided into three lines of five, seven and five.

I was intrigued. Before Sue left, she surprised me with her own book of haikus and her parting words were, "You should write haikus, also!"

I did, and to my amazement, pages and pages of these little poems were about my life at the orphanage. In essence; haiku opened the 'floodgates' for my book.

Traditional haiku will usually include a word pertaining to the season. This, and a few other haiku rules were not known to me at that time. So, my haikus differ, as they reflect my inner thoughts captured in the moment of each situation.

The best way to read a haiku is to return to it several times. Visualize the scene, the feeling and the situation of the writer. Let your thoughts come through and see how they fill in the details and settings, for haiku interacts with the reader to form a 'picture poem.'

The simplicity and the silence of haiku fascinates me. As a poet once said, "Haiku glance, and turn away to think, haiku never stares."

Contents

Chapter 1

Alone I am — Alone I felt

feel the broken heart
see the tear-stained face, and weep
sleep my child, sleep

In 1933, I came into the world amidst great upheaval. The United States of America was in its fourth year of the great depression. Across the nation 14 million were unemployed. Bread lines formed, long-time businesses closed, credit was obsolete and bankruptcy was rampant.

During this turmoil I was born in a small wooden house in Palo Alto, California, a half a block from what is now Riconanda Park. I was the fifth and last child of Chinese immigrant parents. This brief background about my family came from my half- sister when I was a teenager. Those facts are not in my memory, but what is, was the day my childhood was shattered.

That day came without warning. They said it happened because of an emergency. But what that emergency meant was never clear to me, for everything had seemed normal that day in 1935 when I was 2 ½ years of age.

It was morning and as usual my mother and I were in the kitchen of our apartment in San Francisco's Chinatown. Daylight filtered in from the one window in our kitchen and as always I was drawn like a moth to the light. It was the only window in our small two-room apartment and although the view outside was only the side of a building, I always liked this room the best. Mother was fixing breakfast while I played with my toys. (At that time mother and I lived alone. What happened to my siblings is not known to me.) My play area was under the kitchen table so I would be out of her way. Surrounded by table legs and our two dining chairs, I was content in my "pretend house" and would play all morning long.

After breakfast there was a knock on our front door. Mother left the kitchen to enter our dark bedroom and walked around the end of the bed which my mother and I shared, to open the door. The bed dominated the room and when the door opened it nearly touched the middle of the bed. I was always amazed that the door didn't hit the bed.

A stranger entered, a woman I had never seen before. Mother spoke to me in Chinese and said she was taking us for a ride in her car.

I recalled a sense of excitement as mother and I would usually just go for walks. The three of us left the apartment as I held my mother's hand. We stepped into the hallway which was lit with dim yellow lights. There were no sounds from any of the adjacent apartments. The quiet hallway echoed our footsteps. Down the hall we passed a doorway where a mother, baby and a toddler lived. We knew this family as I had been left there twice for short periods while mother was out on errands. As we walked by, I thought, "They don't even know that we are going for a ride." I could visualize mother telling her about our outing, while the woman would say, "Oh, oh," and look at her in awe just like the Chinese women nowadays would do who just came from China. She would be holding her baby upright, close to her heart like she always did and as usual her toddler girl would be clinging to her side.

Even though I was happy to go for a ride, there was no recollection of the long ride to Los Gatos, which in those days without freeways took about two hours. We arrived at the Ming Quong Home, an orphanage for Chinese girls. And the next thing I recall is being in a huge room and I was crying and screaming. For some reason I had been separated from my mother and made to sit on a strange woman's lap. My mother and our driver were standing next to me. I wanted to be out of this stranger's lap and in my mother's arms. But the harder I tried to get away, the tighter the grasp. I felt stifled and out of breath. I stopped my screaming and gulped for air. It was then I noticed a group of women in the middle of the room standing together looking at me. They appeared like looming statues silhouetted against daylight filtered from an adjoining room.

Behind the women was a cluster of young girls who were tense and huddled together and they too were peering at me. No one spoke. It was eerie; they just stared. I looked around and though my eyes were blurred I could see the lights from the glass wall lamps which glowed on the wood-paneled walls.

I wondered, what was I doing in this room? I wanted to leave this place and go home.

Desperately I reached out for my mother, but couldn't quite reach her. "Ma mah," I cried. There was no reply. I was terrified; that was not like her. Again, I pleaded, "Ma mah." She looked down at me blankly and did not seem to understand my terror.

Moments later, the woman tightened her hold on me and at that same instance, I noticed that my mother had turned and walked out the front door with the driver. A gripping fear welled up inside me; I could not believe my mother had left without me. She had never done that before without an explanation. When she had left me at the neighbor's the first time she had told me she would be back soon. And the second and the last time when I was left there I had begun to fidget and cry, so she had given me a piece of candy and said, "don't cry." And I had stopped, for I always obeyed mother. The candy soothed me and besides, I knew she would be back shortly.

So why did my mother leave me now with complete strangers without an explanation? Pent-up anger burst forth and with all my strength I pushed and tried to pry the woman's arms apart, but nothing happened. Twisting and tugging repeatedly, I attempted to get away and felt my face flush. Once more I had failed.

In one final desperate surge, I unleashed the loudest cry of my life. **"MA MAH!"** while inside my heart was pleading, "please don't leave me."

Suddenly an alarmed face appeared from the top of the stairway from an unlit room below. An older girl had bounded up the stairs to also stare at me. But that didn't matter to me, what mattered was my mother was gone.

And now my exhausted body began to jerk while a new flood of hot tears seared my burning face. And my throat, parched and strained, now became mute.

I looked around the room fearfully. The group of young girls approached me shyly and bent down, their sympathetic faces surrounding me. At that moment I saw one girl's face, her eyes were brimmed with tears. I knew these girls cared and I felt comforted. A small hand reached out and touched me and the soundless jerking of my body began to subside.

It was then that the woman got up and held my hand firmly, leading me upstairs. I didn't want to leave the girls I felt akin to. I looked back at the concerned girls looking up at me through the open wooden banister and once again my body wrenched. If I had not been held, I would have fallen.

Once upstairs, the woman who had never spoken a word proceeded to bathe me quickly and methodically. I trembled and shrank from her hurried motions. I wondered why she was bathing me. I wanted my mother.

"Why couldn't she take care of me?" "Why did she leave me?"

"Did I do something wrong?"

I wondered if she still loved me.

I was limp as a puppet as the woman toweled me dry from head to toe. She dressed me in handmade cotton overalls, (donated by the church ladies) and a pair of brown-laced shoes. With deft hands she trimmed my hair in the traditional rice-bowl style with straight bangs. I now looked like the rest of the girls.

Would my mother recognize me when she came back for me? My bath and new appearance was the last shock of the day. I was overwhelmed and exhausted. I didn't even remember the rest of the day or even going to bed that evening. The only person I knew and loved was gone. I was alone. I had been abandoned.

That day I became the youngest child ever to be admitted to the Ming Quong orphanage; the usual acceptance age was 5 years.

And 60 years later, Luella, the 10-year-old girl who had been on kitchen duty that day and had bounded up the stairs to witness my abandonment, told me how she had never forgotten that day or that scream. She had never heard anything like that before. She added that chills had shot through her body followed by her own physical chest pains.

She was also able to tell me what my mother wore. She said she wore a black hat — the type that hugged the head for warmth — and that she had on a black Chinese top with a high collar which fastened on the side.

And Luella's next statement shocked me. She said, "I remember your grandma, because she dressed just the way my grandma dressed!"

My grandma? Shocked as I was, I didn't contradict Luella then, because I knew in my mind, that the woman who had brought me to the orphanage had been my mother.

So from Luella's account of that painful day, my mother (who was probably in her 30s) was dressed in the manner of an aged woman!

Chapter 2

Without a Mother's Love

out of the womb — cries
survival sounds heard clearly
lifeline severed twice

The days that followed were lost and hazy. I was too homesick to notice anything, but when the older girls, who were 5 to 8 years older than me, held my hand and walked with me, I felt better.

"Come on Nona," they'd gently coax. "Don't you want to go on the swing? We'll push you."

I didn't answer. I would just stare at them and keep my distance. I don't know how many weeks or months passed before I began to warm up, but finally when the patient girls succeeded in lifting me into the bucket swing, the fresh air fanned my face, while the swing's motion began to soothe and relax my body. Soon the corners of my mouth rose. The girls responded gleefully. Their happiness made me smile even more. These girls were nice; they cared for me, they liked me.

They called out, "Like it Nona?" I nodded.

"Want to go higher?" "Yes," I cried.

"Hang on," they yelled.

Zooming higher and higher my swing caught up with the other swings in use, and our laughter filled the Home's entire playground.

As time passed I slowly began to familiarize myself with the routine of this large household, of 35 girls and five teachers.

About two months later, I woke one morning to the ringing of a loud bell. Where was I? One sleepy eye opened and I could not see the familiar walls of my

17

bedroom in San Francisco and realized I was still at the orphanage. I couldn't believe I was still here. It was a Monday morning. I realized it was 6:30, time to get up, but I lay motionless as persistent rings cleared my groggy mind. I feigned sleep, for I knew if I stirred the girl across the way from me would call out, "Get up Nona." I wanted this brief time to think about my mother.

Yesterday had been visiting day and like many other Sundays the visiting period had come and gone without an appearance from her.

I sighed. Didn't she know I missed her and yearned for her comforting ways?

Ming Quong Home (Former Spreckles Estate)

A tear spilled out one eye and tickled my ear, but I didn't move. If only she could comfort me now. But I knew when mother came to visit, everything would be all right, for she would take me home.

But before we left, I would show her this big house.

We would start at the main building which was cement

stucco and had massive square pillars which held up the second story of dark shingle exterior with a porch that wrapped around the whole house. She would see the unusual front door made of glass and covered with gauze. We would enter a small foyer and on each side she would see two ornate ceramic elephants on either side of the door. Beneath our feet, we would feel the soft plush of an Oriental rug, its rich colors of cobalt and deep tangerine glistening like velvet. Before us was the wooden stairway which led up to the area, (which was formally a porch) where my group, called the Nursery, slept. There were

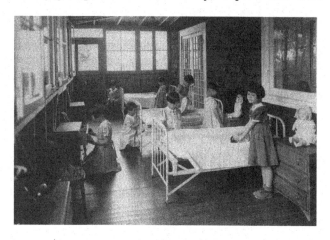

Nursery Group

seven of us, ages 5 to 6 and our teacher's name was Miss Chew. I would point out my bed in the corner closest to Miss Chew's bedroom, because I was the youngest. I would also tell mother that the rough wood and exposed 2 x 4's sometimes scared me, for at nap time big spiders scurried across the walls. I knew she would be alarmed. She'd reassure me and I'd feel better. She would be amazed at the quiet surroundings and listen to all the birds chirping; I knew she would smile. Her gaze would be directed to the windows framed with an old oak tree, which I loved.

We would continue on to the second group of girls called the Starlights. Their sleeping quarters was a continuation of our porch. These girls were 7 to 9 years old and their teacher was Miss Davies. Heading downstairs we would pass the large reception room. This room was divided into three sections by the arrangement of furniture. In one corner stood an oversized wooden bench with a high carved back. In the center of the room, cushioned rattan chairs and a couch were grouped on a large Oriental rug in front of a brick fireplace. And at the end of the room two large conversation chairs were in front of a picture window with a built-in cushioned seat. Right off this room we would enter the Chinese classroom, where round tables of varying heights for each group was used. Then through a connecting French door, we'd peer into the living room. I couldn't wait to see her expression, as this was the most beautiful room in the house, complete with a large picture window overlooking Santa Clara Valley, with San Jose on the distant horizon.

After that bright room we'd go down a long flight of stairs to the dark playroom, which was below ground level. Small, narrow windows bordered the entire top of two walls and if someone outside walked by all we could see from this level were their legs! Cubby holes lined one wall with one cube for each girl. I would direct her to my cubby hole and show her all my treasures that I had found from nature, such as a pretty leaf, a shiny acorn and some spent flowers.

Adjacent to the playroom was the sunny white kitchen. Miss Reber, the cook who was always busy, would still find time to look our way and smile. I would tell mother that when the rest of the girls were attending the public schools, Miss Reber and I would grocery shop.

Once outside we would pass the infirmary, (which was used as the Spreckles' caretaker's house) which was off-limits to us. But I would describe to mother that the quarantined room used for contagious diseases, like measles or mumps was decorated with a wallpaper of Mickey Mouse and Donald Duck. It was too bad I couldn't show her that room, because she probably didn't know about those cartoon characters.

Across the front yard, near the rose garden stood a converted dark-shingled building, (which had been a barn). Nestled amidst the hay on the ground floor, the Home's car was parked. The upstairs housed the third group of 10-11 year olds. Their teacher, Mrs. Lee named her group of girls, "Lok-Hin", (the joy-givers.) She had even made up a special song for them in Chinese and English, titled, "We are little joy-givers of Ming Quong."

Alongside the Lok-Hin quarters was the smallest building called the Cottage. About six older girls, usually around 12 years of age and up, roomed there by themselves with no teacher. They were the lucky ones! Because as Rhoda, a cottage girl, said, "we could talk all night and sometimes even play Monopoly (with our flashlights) until we got caught by a passing teacher!"

By now, I knew my mother would need a rest, so I would quickly point out the playground equipped with two sturdy wooden teeter-totters, climbing bars, swings, a giant slide and two deserted barn houses which we now used for playing house.

Scampering across the way I would take her hand and lead her to the flower garden filled with all kinds of trees and different pathways. At the end of one path partially hidden from view was a stone gazebo, which we called the "ding-dong bell." Here we would rest inside the cool gazebo surrounded by the perfume of cascading lavender wisteria and occasional bees.

Looking out the gazebo we would be able to see the entrance to the Home graced with a towering gate where a sign, Ming Quong Home in antique gold hung. This gate stood alongside majestic pine trees, which mother never saw in Chinatown.

Every time I walked under that open gate, the wing-tipped beams reminded me of the big black birds which often circled above in the vivid blue sky. I would ask her if she thought it resembled a bird also.

Suddenly out of nowhere a shrill voice broke through my reverie. "Get up sleepy-head."

Startled, I realized the Nursery girls were up and trooping by my bed to get to Miss Chew's warm bedroom to get dressed. I jumped out of bed, grabbed my carefully laid-out clothes from my chair and followed them.

Miss Chew was brushing a girl's hair and warned, "Hurry girls, only 15 minutes before the second bell." She looked at me and asked, "Did you over-sleep this morning, Nona?"

"No," I answered, as I dressed quickly.

By the time the bell sounded, we were ready to head downstairs to the dining room.

Then I remembered I forgot to show mother the dining room and realized why. In order to go to the dining room, one had to walk through a pitch-black passageway connecting the playroom to the dining room, and although it was a short walkway it was spooky. That area contained the household utilities and one could hear the water heater and pilot light sounds and see flickers of light going on and off. So it was better that she didn't see it, but she missed seeing the white dining room with our six round tables, wooden stools and the regular chairs for the teachers.

And now in the playroom we were all lined up, including the teachers, waiting for the third bell to ring. We could smell the fragrant slices of crisp toast Miss Reber with the assistance of an older girl had baked in the oven. But best of all the tantalizing aroma of hot chocolate filled the room.

As the bell sounded each person headed towards their designated table and stood behind their stool. When everyone was in place, we bowed our heads and closed our eyes while a teacher said the morning prayer out loud, "Thanking God for the food and the beginning of another day." We always had a prayer before each meal.

We ate quickly as each girl had a household chore to do before school. My job was dusting the Nursery's dressers and chairs. Miss Chew had taught me to poke a finger through a cloth to dust between each rung.

Through with breakfast, I asked, "Miss Chew, may I please be excused?" Granted permission, I carefully and slowly carried my dishes out to the kitchen table and stacked them with the other dirty dishes. I placed my utensils in a large pan filled with water for soaking.

Heading upstairs, I mused, life here was so different, punctuated by bells and so full of rules. But there was no time to ponder that now for as soon as my first household job was done, a second one awaited me and I dare not be late!

Chapter 3

Miss Chew

helping hands reach out
eyes of terror — change to trust
balanced life is shared

"Good-bye, good-bye," I called as the girls ran down the hill to school. They returned my calls, some waving with their lunch bags. I hollered and waved until the last girl was out of sight. Every morning it was the same routine, after their departure an emptiness washed over me. Where just minutes ago the yard had been filled with voices, now there was complete silence. I felt like the sun and the sky and I were the only ones left in the world. But I was not afraid, I was just lonely, for now there were no girls to play with or to fuss over me.

To many of the girls, I was like their living doll. Sometimes they'd tie big bows in my hair while laughing with glee. Their maternal instincts were lavished on me which I enjoyed, though sometimes felt over-whelmed. They said I was cute with a round face and big eyes.

At times when they doted over me, they often said something that puzzled me. It was never said maliciously, it was their thoughts and feelings shared amongst themselves I was the "teacher's pet." Every time I heard that remark, I thought it was strange as the teachers never treated me differently. In actuality it was really the older girls who favored me. Because I was not of school age I was put in the care of whomever was available and they had to take me with them and in that respect I was treated

in a special way. But I never made a comment, because I knew it wasn't true. I knew the teachers liked me because I was well behaved. My short time with mother had prepared me well. But there was one incident I found out about as an adult which could have prompted that comment.

There was a kindly caretaker at the Home named Mr. Torrey. And as he related to me, "I took a liking to him and he to me." Each time I saw him, I would say, "Hello, Mr. MacCorrey."

And no matter how hard I tried to say Torrey, it came out MacCorrey, much to his amusement.

San Jose Rose Garden
w/Mr Torrey's Parents & Miss Chew

One day while the girls were in school, he planned an outing for Miss Chew and I, which included his parents. On his day off he drove us all to the rose garden in San Jose.

From the pictures Mr. Torrey took that day, we were all dressed in our Sunday best. Even Miss Chew, whom I'd never seen wearing a hat, had one on for this occasion.

Looking back, this special outing would of course have seemed like favoritism.

I remember a time the girls and I were outside in the front yard. We were seated on the stone bench under the pepper tree. The girls were combing my hair, when one piped, "Do you know why you came to the Home?"

Surprised and a little sad, I said, "No, I don't, why?" "Because," she replied casually, "It was an emergency and you were really not old enough, but they let you in anyways."

"Who told you?" I questioned.

"Miss Reber told us." And the other girls' faces

indicated that they also knew. I thought they were brave to ask a teacher this question, because that was not the thing to do and besides the teachers always seemed to evade any of the girls' questions. It was common knowledge not to ask about our past. We were expected to accept our lives' situations. But the girls felt safe asking Miss Reber, who was friendly and approachable and besides, she wasn't a "regular" teacher (because there were no girls under her care). Yet when the girls asked her again about my emergency, she said she'd forgotten. Disappointed I accepted Miss Reber's answer.

The heartfelt pain I felt for my mother gradually subsided and was replaced with a dull ache. Yet life here was not full of sadness. We passed the days in continuous play, oftentimes playing "house" and fantasizing the "ideal family," always complete with a mother and father.

Nona (in front) with older girls.

Now when I thought of mother, Miss Chew came to mind. I felt the closest to her, but unlike mother she did not show any outward affection. Miss Chew was a tiny, strong-willed woman, who rarely smiled. Her black hair was always neatly rolled up above her nape. Small, wire-rimmed glasses framed her often serious eyes. She was strict, fair and rather kind and spoke only when necessary.

I thought of her strict ways and involuntarily let out a

gasp.

My second job! I hoped I was not late.

Just then a voice rang out, "Nona, it's time to go to work."

I looked up and saw Miss Chew from the open window of the Nursery's quarters. Sprinting, I cried, "Yes, Miss Chew, I'm coming."

Once upstairs, I could see Miss Chew piling the dirty clothes into the large bamboo basket. I waited till she was through and followed behind her as she carried the clothes down flights of steep stairs passed the Chinese classroom on her way to the laundry room. She balanced her heavy basket with both hands and managed to open the swinging screen door, with one foot. Trying to keep up with Miss Chew's rapid pace took all my energy, but I knew soon I would be able to hold the door open as she came zooming by.

The laundry room was devoid of windows and was dark and foreboding. It was like a dungeon with walls of jagged rocks, festered with hunks of concrete. Inside a thin shaft of light poured through a crack in a far corner. A naked bulb dangled from the low ceiling and when Miss Chew tugged on the pulley the light cast eerie shadows against the walls. I was glad I was with Miss Chew. Large connecting tubs lined one wall of the room. At the end of these deep tubs, nickel scrub boards were stacked to be used by the older girls. Each girl was assigned a day to do their wash, the same procedure was done for their ironing day.

At the other end a round washing machine was reserved only for Miss Chew. Now as she filled the tub with clothes, hot water and soap, I stood on my tippy toes and watched as the clear steamy water became cloudy and the waxy odor of soap invaded my nostrils. My eyes were as big as the tub of water swishing back and forth. I could feel Miss Chew watching me as my eyes followed the rhythm of the swirling water. She could hardly keep from smiling. I'd gasp in awe and purse my lips as each shimmering bubble danced about and burst.

Looking up at Miss Chew I'd watch her smile fade. It seemed maybe she didn't want me to see her smile as it would make her vulnerable.

After the wash, the clothes would be put into adjacent cement tubs and rinsed twice. As she worked swiftly, beads of perspiration surfaced on her forehead. The clothes went through the hand wringer and emerged flat and matted together. Eagerly I tried to pry the stiff clothes apart, but to no avail. Miss Chew as usual took over and with one big flap they fell apart. We sorted them into piles of socks, underpants, shirts and overalls. In one small pile were white cotton handkerchiefs that Miss Chew had cut from old bed sheets. I thought she was so clever to use a pinking shear with zigzag cutters to turn ordinary hankies into fancy ones with rick-rack edges.

When the clean clothes piled up to her chin she had to carefully tilt the basket sideways down some narrow steps to go outside. Trailing behind her, I'd watch to see if anything dropped. If that happened, I'd call out, "Miss Chew, you dropped something." No response. I'd pick it up and run to catch up with her.

We emerged outdoors into the bright sunlight where two long squeaky pulley lines stood. Working swiftly, I would find the mate for each sock. Then with my hands stretched as far as I could reach, I'd have 2 straight wooden clothespins ready for her to grasp.

After many months of my helping Miss Chew with the wash, there were times when she seemed to forget I was there. I noticed her eyes were really sad, almost watery and her mind seemed to be miles away. I would wonder about her.

I knew that on her dresser a silver frame held a picture of a gracious woman. Each morning when Miss Chew brushed my hair, I would gaze at this photograph. It always filled me with a good feeling.

29

This woman, I later learned was Emma Mills, a teacher at a mission in San Francisco Chinatown called "920." "Nine- twenty" was the house number and like the Los Gatos home, they were also sponsored and run by the Occidental (Presbyterian) National Board of Missions.

In the 1800s during the era of San Francisco's Barbary Coast this mission once sheltered needy Chinese girls and immigrant girls from China who had been forced into the trade of household slavery or prostitution. These girls had been enticed, kidnapped or oftentimes sold by their poverty stricken families in China by a small group of Chinese men with assistance from Caucasian men in this country.

At age 3, Miss Chew had been abandoned by a Chinese foster mother fleeing from a vicious San Francisco Chinatown tong war. A tong war in the 1800s was made up of warring Chinese groups, each trying to control Chinatown's unsavory activities that would make money. The Kwong Dak Tong trafficked in girls and the Hip Shing Tong ran the gambling joints. All manner of weapons were used in their mortal fights, but the hatchet became the most notorious one, resulting in the term, "the hatchet men."

A terrified Chinese neighbor left Miss Chew at the doorstep of "920" and the legendary Donaldina Cameron, the director of the Mission, rescued Miss Chew and she was raised as one of Miss Cameron's "daughters." She became a favorite of Miss Cameron's as she was dependable with a carefree personality.

Two years later, on April 18, 1906, when Miss Chew was 5 years old, the massive San Francisco earthquake rocked Northern California, sending everyone at the Mission scrambling for what they could carry. Miss Chew was given the delicate task of carrying a basket of two dozen eggs, which she did willingly anticipating eating them later. Because this earthquake of an 8.2 magnitude literally wrecked the city, all San Franciscans had to concentrate on putting their lives together and as a result the tong wars of 20 years finally came to an end.

> *Note: The word tong is commonly associated with gang activities because the racketeers back then adopted this term. But tong in Chinese simply means "association" or "meeting place." Tong was therefore a term attached to many Chinese organizations without involvement in violence of any kind. Tongs were also created for protection from the family, in the interest of family surnames.*
>
> *Most of them were started in America and accepted Chinese people from all walks of life.*
>
> *The tongs are male dominated, the women rarely participate in the social structure of the family association. Back then there were more tongs, but now there are only five tongs on the West Coast and two in the East Coast.*

Growing up Miss Chew considered life as "one big joke." Miss Chew in her short time had already experienced a lifetime of terror and loneliness.

Many times she witnessed terrified girls who had been rescued by Donaldina Cameron and hidden in the tunnels (the coal bins) of "920," while their angry former owners stormed the premises looking for their lost property.

During this era another fear was the thought of being kidnapped and forced into this degrading life. (Even decades after this problem subsided any brave women tourists who dared to venture into Chinatown were on the alert.)

As a dependable 14-year-old, Miss Chew was sent to Oakland to care for nine young girls at the Tooker Home, (an offshoot of "920".) In 1915, the Tooker Home was named after two sisters who donated the large two-story house. Miss Chew missed her good friends, but at least there was less fear of kidnapping in the East bay.

As Miss Chew's life became balanced, she vowed when she grew up she would come back to the Mission and help out wherever she was needed.

Miss Chew studied Home Economics at the Santa Barbara Teachers College, and also at the Los Angeles Bible Institute. During this time she mostly supported herself, but with the help of $10.00 a month from Miss Cameron and her assistant, which she did not want to accept.

In 1927, her vision became a reality. She returned to San Francisco and became a staff member of "920," once even assisting Miss Cameron along with another teacher in rescuing a baby sold by its father from a brothel in Locke, California.

As more girls entered the Mission, it was of utmost concern to separate the "innocent girls" from the "girls whose innocence had been destroyed," because the worldly slave girls bitterness might influence the younger girl's outlook on life.

A site next to the Mills College campus in Oakland, California was found.

Emma Mills, (the woman in the photo on Miss Chew's dresser) was the director. Along with other teachers, Miss Chew was transferred to that Ming Quong Home. She was a tremendous help to Miss Mills. (Emma Mills was of no relation to Mills College).

As times changed, the teachers felt the older girls needed to be closer to Oakland's Chinatown in order to be part of the Chinese community. Also, many of the younger girls were sickly and a sunnier location was desirable.

In agreement with Mills College, a site near Lake Merritt and a large home with four and a half acres in sunny Los Gatos was traded. The former owners of this estate was the Spreckles sugar family who lost this home because of the depression.

In 1934, a year before I arrived, Miss Chew was transferred to the new Home in Los Gatos. After learning about Miss Chew's incredible background, I could understand her sad and distant manner and what she must have been thinking about the day of my arrival when she first cared for me.

.   .   .

And now, working with Miss Chew each morning, I'd always feel good, because I knew I had been of help. I'd gaze proudly at the clothes flapping in the clear breeze, while I waited for Miss Chew to speak. And when she finally spoke, the morning's quiet was broken by her all familiar words, "That's all now Nona, you can go play."

And as usual, I would reply, "Thank you, Miss Chew." Although Miss Chew always taught us to say "thank you," she never said it to me for that was the order of things. I was the child, she was the teacher and that was my job.

Chapter 4

The Cook and the Creme Puff

kind-hearted teacher
whose love brimmed gold and silver
shared sweets between us

"Nona, Nona where are you?" I could hear Miss Reber calling me, but I couldn't answer; I was in the playground swinging from the Nursery's iron bars. I was practicing my swings and loops. I still could not master them like the other agile girls.

I jumped down quickly and rushed up to the front yard, where I knew

Miss Reber would be patiently waiting by the car, for today was grocery shopping day.

"Hi Miss Reber, I'm here," I greeted.

Nursery Bars

Miss Reber looked at me kindly and asked, "Do you have to go to the bathroom?"

"No, Miss Reber."

"Okay then, jump in."

I scrambled into the Home's new wood-paneled station wagon and as Miss Reber closed the door, she warned me as usual, "Watch out for your fingers." And as usual, I quickly placed my hands on my lap. I loved these outings and felt privileged to be with her.

Miss Chew, Miss Reber

Miss Reber had fair skin, with brown hair and soft curls and was slightly heavy. She wore reading glasses which usually slid down her fine chiseled nose. She had a degree in Home Economics, but because of the depression, she could not find a job in her related field. A friend had told her of the job opening at Ming Quong.

Miss Reber was also our piano player. Her beautiful black, lacquered piano sat in its own alcove in the living room.

On Saturdays after dinner, the whole home gathered in the living room for prayer time and singing. This was special, as on weekdays we were with our own age group. Many times our prayer time together would turn into a songfest with girls calling out the page number of their favorite hymn before another girl had a chance. Occasionally an over-exuberant girl would yell out even before the song was finished. Everyone wanted to laugh, but we restrained ourselves as that was not proper. The embarrassed one would blush, while we giggled silently.

I love to watch Miss Reber's cheerful expression and would marvel at her nimble fingers flying across the keys. How I long to play the piano like her.

On weekdays Miss Reber and I always shopped in the same grocery store for fruits and vegetables. The owner, a balding man who always wore a grey muted stripe shirt and brown pants was there and always had a friendly smile for me. I could hear my name mentioned in his conversations with Miss Reber. He thought I was cute.

Once he asked me if I wanted a banana. I shook my head slowly back and forth in reply. He then offered candy. I looked at Miss Reber for approval and she nodded her head. With trepidation, I held out my hand, took the lollipop and shyly put it in my mouth. The man's face broke out into a smile that caused me to draw closer to Miss Reber. I knew I should thank him because we were taught to do that, but I remained silent. Miss Reber patiently waited for my response and finally said, "What do you say, Nona?" And I said, "Thank you." Normally, I would just look at him and not utter a word. When Miss Reber was through shopping, I'd turn and look back at him and he'd still have that smile across his face. I was glad to leave. From then on, every time we shopped there he would give me a lollipop.

When Miss Reber and I walked around this quaint town, curious glances came our way. To them I must have looked like a refuge just off the boat from China and of course Miss Reber didn't look like my mother! Ladies would stop us and ask my name. I was the only Chinese in this town populated by Northern

Europeans. I'd cling to Miss Reber's side and look up at the ladies with their brimmed hats which shadowed their inquisitive eyes. Miss Reber was amused. But what made her chuckle was the day she was walking so fast, I had to run to catch up with her. Some concerned women who were behind us called out, "Don't walk so fast!" When I caught up with her, she joked, "Am I walking your little legs off?"

I looked at my legs and wondered what she meant. Every so often Miss Reber and I would stop in a wonderful sweet-smelling bakery. The clean white bakery had 3 glass showcases of the most interesting desserts I'd ever seen.

One day when she was ordering, I knelt down and stared in amazement at the gigantic creme puffs filled with mountains of whipped cream. To my surprise, she asked, "Would you like that Nona?" I was so startled I could hardly respond. I nodded yes, but I really had my eye on a cookie. I didn't want to hurt her feelings so I grinned and took a bite. The cream squished out all over my face, much to Miss Reber's delight. I didn't like it, although I never showed my distaste. I had never tasted whipped cream and its richness overwhelmed me. Feeling my stomach turn, I could barely swallow my mouthful. Laughing, Miss Reber helped me and asked if I wanted another bite. I said, "no," and watched with relief as she finished the rich dessert.

Once when I wasn't feeling well, I was transferred from the Nursery sleeping quarters to the infirmary, which was adjacent to Miss Reber's bedroom. As Miss Reber emerged from her room, I could see she was carrying her black handbag. I pined, "Miss Reber are you going shopping now?"

"Yes, Nona."

"I wish I could go with you."

"I know, Nona, but you have to rest and get well. I'll be back soon."

A tear ran out of the corner of my eye.

"Go to sleep, Nona. You'll feel better soon." I turned around in bed and watched her leave.

Sobbing silently, I closed my eyes. The next thing I became aware of was Miss Reber standing beside my bed holding a box. She was back already? I was surprised.

I must have fallen asleep.

She presented me with the box. "For me?" I asked incredulously.

She smiled and nodded.

Eagerly I sat up and quickly opened the box. Inside was another gigantic creme puff! I looked at her happy face and didn't know what to do, but I did smile and thank her.

As soon as she left for the kitchen to prepare dinner, I rushed to the bathroom and threw the creme puff in the

37

toilet and pulled down on the pulley. I was so afraid it would not go down and that Miss Reber might come back. What a relief, as I watched the strong swirl of rushing water flush it completely away.

This was the first surprise I remembered receiving and I felt confused and guilty. I wondered if I should have told Miss Reber the truth, but I didn't want to make her sad. Frustrated with myself, I at least knew one thing for sure — Miss Reber was the kindest teacher at the Home.

Chapter 5

Our Neighbor

*a lone man's sorrow
hidden deeply in his soul
leaves aching silence*

Every morning after work (as we called it) we had to go outdoors to play. We could never stay inside unless the weather was bad and if it was, permission had to be granted first. The only time we were permitted inside was to use the bathroom or to get a toy.

On this particular Saturday, (when I was around 3 ½ years old) I carefully closed the playroom door quietly behind me, for I was aware of Miss Reber's poor aching ears from hearing hundreds of slammed doors throughout the day.

I trudged up the ramp to ground level and headed toward the playground. As I drew closer to the Lok-Hin building, I noticed a group of girls gathered around some kind of cage. Mr. Sawyer (name has been changed to protect identity of any living relatives), our grizzly looking neighbor who always wore heavy overalls and sturdy work shoes was beside the cage.

"Come on, Nona," someone yelled. "Come

see Mr. Sawyer's twin baby goats."

I pressed in eagerly next to the excited girls and squealed with delight as I peeked into the dark narrow openings of their large wooden cage. I had never seen baby goats and to see twins was even more exciting.

I could smell the fresh hay and watched them eat. I was completely fascinated as they munched each bite. Each strand of straw jerked up and

Twin Goats Miss Bankes, Nona

down and back and forth till it disappeared into their hungry mouths. When they were through, they nudged their funny noses up to our curious faces and "baahed."

We screamed in surprise and clamored, "They want more food."

Laughing Mr. Sawyer roared, "There's no more hay."

We looked beseechingly at him and cried, "But they're still hungry." He laughed again and retorted, "Well then, pull some weeds."

"Weeds?" we chorused.

"They'll eat anything," Mr. Sawyer replied.

We didn't want the goats to go hungry, so we pulled handfuls of sour grass and milkweeds and crammed them through the cage. They devoured it. Their favorite was the milkweeds which oozed a white milky substance causing our fingers to stick and reek of a bitter odor. But we didn't mind and we continued to feed them milkweeds till their little stomachs bulged.

I remember vividly the first encounter with our neighbor. We had been in the playground and some older girls had been playing catch when the ball suddenly flew over our neighbor's yard. Through the loose wire fence that defined our property line, we could see Mr. Sawyer in his yard. He retrieved our ball and threw it back to us. The girls thanked him. He stood there with a curious expression and asked us if we were Chinese. "Yes," we replied. He then asked us all our names and was curious why so many of us lived here together. We told him we had no parents. "You're orphans?" he questioned. The older girls hesitated as if hearing that word for the first time, but nodded in accordance. He couldn't believe it, so he began to question each of us individually. As each girl quipped "yes" or "no," his astonished jaws dropped, which made us laugh. We could tell that he didn't believe us. So we cried out, "It's true, it's true. Go ahead and ask some more girls."

And soon his questioning became like a game with each participant feeling the impact their answers had on him. We felt a sadness within him.

That day I had been sitting on the Nursery swing and he looked my way and asked, "Do you have a mother?" "Yes," I answered shyly. "And you have a father?" "No," I replied rather boastful like, for even though I was the youngest, I could still participate. I felt a strong kinship with the girls because I was one of them and I knew the answers. But to my surprise my answers made the man's face even funnier-looking, which in turn bought more laughter from us.

We then asked him what his name was and I recalled his hardy laugh. "Mr. Sawyer," he boomed. He then introduced us to his daughters who during this entire bantering had been standing shyly by his side.

Mr. Sawyer's sharing had been a wonderful surprise as we rarely saw our closest neighbor. Their house was located in the farthest corner of the playground on a knoll, with a forest of tall eucalyptus trees surrounding his house. But even if their house had been closer we would still not have known them any better because they kept to themselves. His wife and two young daughters who were in grade school were unusually quiet and withdrawn. The sisters appeared to be fearful of everything; they rarely smiled or laughed like us.

I remember one morning on the way to school, (when I was around 9 years old) I saw the younger sister who was in my class walking behind us. I stopped and called out, "Want to walk with us?" That startled her and she didn't answer. We waited. She hesitated with a confused expression on her face. We continued on, while she lagged behind keeping her distance. I felt sorry for her. Maybe she missed her sister who generally walked with her.

It was their gregarious father who instigated any activities for us girls.

I recalled during the summer Miss Bankes (who was head of the home at that time) announced that Mr. Sawyer was going to Santa Cruz with his family and invited some girls to go. Miss Bankes asked for a raise of hands from just the older girls who might be interested in going. Of course, all hands shot up, so Miss Bankes had to pick which girls were the best suited for this particular outing. We were so envious. A day at the ocean, the famous Boardwalk, and the exciting Giant Dipper, which was the largest roller coaster in the world. We heard that the Santa Cruz Boardwalk was the most fun and exciting place to go.

But the next time Mr. Sawyer invited the girls to go again, no one volunteered! For no one had told Miss Bankes what had occurred on that trip and no one wanted to tell her. But Miss Bankes got to the bottom of it and found out that Mr. Sawyer had taken the treacherous curves on Highway 17 like a madman. The girls were terrified and some became nauseated.

But because Miss Bankes could not go back on her word a few girls were forced to go. And this time one of the girls actually threw up! And that ended the invites!

One day while we were outside playing kickball, our ball flew over the fence and landed in the Sawyer's yard. Mr. Sawyer did not hear our constant cries of, "Mr. Sawyer could you please give us our ball?" With permission from a teacher inside the house, we walked up to the Sawyer's house to retrieve our ball.

Upon entering their front yard, I was intrigued immediately. In the middle of a circular driveway was a giant redwood tree which dwarfed their modest Berkeley-style house. Incredible century plants zoomed upwards while their large base spread out like octopus tentacles.

We found Mr. Sawyer in an open shed milking a nanny goat. The procedure looked painful and so bizarre. The nanny's udder was so full it nearly touched the ground. We had watched in repulsion mixed with curiosity as he pulled and squeezed the drooping nipples. He reassured us he wasn't hurting the nanny and then he looked up at our pained faces and asked, "Have you ever had goat's ice cream?" We made a face and cried, "Yuck!" Who would want to eat it and besides we didn't really believe him. He laughed and posed a second question. "Do you know what ice cream is made of?" We looked at him blankly. And when he said, it was from cow's milk, we gasped in horror.

Mr. Sawyer said, "You don't believe me, do you?" We didn't answer. And then he said, "I'll prove it to you."

A few days later Miss Bankes unexpectedly announced that the whole Home was invited to the Sawyer's for dinner. We were so excited. We couldn't believe it, Mr. Sawyer had kept his word. Of course the teachers never knew what prompted the dinner invitation.

At the Home we never ate out, so this invitation was a big event.

That evening, hot dogs with all the trimmings were laid out before us and we picnicked in his yard. We loved this new type of sandwich which was never on the Home's menu. We politely stuffed ourselves with second and even third helpings! Anticipating the dessert, Mr. Sawyer told us wholeheartedly that we were going to have ice cream just as soon as we made it!

Our jaws dropped. Did that mean we had to milk the nanny also? With great trepidation we all followed Mr. Sawyer to the shed and there waiting for us was a small, round wooden tub with a wooden plunger. We could see with relief that the tub was already filled with goat's milk. Mr. Sawyer told us all we had to do was push the plunger up and down and ice cream would appear.

"That's all?" we questioned.

"That's right," he laughed as he walked away.

We took turns plunging till we were exhausted. It never thickened! We had no idea it would be so much work. The older girls worked harder and faster, when finally it showed some signs of thickening.

We ran off to find Mr. Sawyer and found him and his family seated on chaise lounge chairs beneath the shade of their majestic tree. He was the only one chatting with the teachers, while his family listened. We waited impatiently for a chance to speak.

"Excuse us, Mr. Sawyer, we would like to know if the ice cream is ready."

He winked mischievously at the teachers and dismissed himself.

Looking down at the tub he bellowed up at us, "No, churn some more."

And we did, when finally to our amazement the milk hardened and clung to the plunger. This time it really looked like real ice cream.

Mr. Sawyer scooped out the dessert. Still skeptical,

44

we hesitated. His commanding voice rang out, "Eat your ice cream!" We looked at the teachers for reassurance, which wasn't there. We were on our own! Finally adventurous Edna (who was the Home's tomboy) tried a spoonful. We waited and she took another mouthful and we followed. "Hmmm," I thought, it was different, like regular ice cream, but with a strong flavor."

Laughing, Mr. Sawyer boomed, "Want some more?" "Yeah," we clamored. Even the teachers appeared to enjoy the ice cream, though none of them had seconds. Only a joyous Miss Reber had another scoop. We felt Miss Reber's adventure- some spirit, but we also realized that tonight was the first time Miss Reber could just sit back and enjoy someone else's cooking!

And that memorable day our neighbor had made his point. Leaving for home, we thanked him profusely.

With a giant smile, he asked, "Now do you believe me about the other kind of ice cream?" We were puzzled, and he bellowed, "Remember what I told you about the cow's milk, that's what ice cream is made of."

"Oh," we giggled. He was right. Our neighbor was a smart man. And we never doubted his word again.

Throughout the years the hypnotic droning of Mr. Sawyer's tractor at naptime played like a lullaby lulling me to sleep. I loved the sound of the tractor trudging uphill, knowing that his laboring tractor broke the heavy clouts of dirt between the endless rolls of fruit trees. The sound would fade as he continued down the other side of the hill and everything in the countryside was once again silent, except for the familiar haunting cries of the quails. But like a faithful geyser the tractor reappeared once again and drummed its way into our naps.

But one day the sound stopped . . .

Miss Reber, who had been in the kitchen, heard the crack of a splitting gunshot which came from the direction of the Sawyer's orchard.

Fragmented whispers by the older girls was that Mr.

Sawyer had committed suicide. But what the hidden words, "committed suicide" meant, I didn't understand then. But I was aware that it was bad, as a dark and sullen mood prevailed whenever the words were said.

The teachers never mentioned it and the older girls said no more. It was simply not for us little ones to know.

As the long summer days merged into the different seasons, our life continued as before with one exception. Miss Bankes announced that any balls falling into our neighbor's yard were to remain there, as we were not to bother the Sawyer's anymore and make a nuisance of ourselves.

And now after all these years all communications with our neighbors were to be severed! I did not understand. My heart ached, but Miss Bankes' word was law and no one dared to question her new rule.

Sometime later when the ball once again flew over the fence, we remembered Miss Bankes strict orders and we moaned and groaned. But some girls ran up and down the whole length of the property line, (which was close to three football fields) looking for some opening or hole. They found one! Halfway down the middle of the property a tiny hole was located close to the ground and Edna slithered through amidst silent cheers!

During the years when I lived at the Los Gatos orphanage two administrators (head of the Home as was our terminology) were in charge at separate times. Miss Bankes was first, followed by Miss Hayes. Other short term teachers were Miss Calecod, Mrs. Lum, Mrs. Barnhart and a nurse, Miss Laurence, followed by another young nurse. Also a few short-term girls, some who came just for the summer, swelled the household count to 40 or more. A monthly charge for each girl's stay was $50.00 a month with a sliding scale of *what a relative could afford. Any unpaid balance was subsidized by the Board of Missions.*

The teachers were usually paid $20.00 a month with room and board.

Chapter 6

A Playmate

girls caught up in play
fantasies expressed with joy
heart to heart with love

I was so excited when Carol came to the Home, because like me she was a preschooler; now I finally had a playmate. Carol was petite and cute, but she had long shiny raised scars across both thighs. She told us her mother had tied her to a bedpost while she went to work. That horrified us.

Nursery group: names mentioned are in book.
Front middle: Nona, Carol on right;
2nd row: Jenny, Frances

In my mind I could see Carol's little face crying and straining for her mother. It was hard for us to understand why Carol loved her mother so much despite her abuse.

After Carol had lived with us for some time, one

summer during school vacation, we took swimming lessons at the town's local pool. In order to receive a certificate of completion one had to jump off the diving board. Everyone jumped and when it was Carol's turn she stood at the edge of the diving board petrified. We couldn't understand what was wrong with her. We repeatedly coaxed her and even when the patient instructor got in the pool and reassured her, "I'll be right here to catch you," she wouldn't budge.

We tried another tactic, "Jump Carol or you won't get a certificate." But she remained motionless with her head bent forward and both hands clasped tightly around her chest. She shivered pathetically and I could see her tormented face. I felt such empathy for her. Later while walking home she shared her thoughts with us. She thought if she jumped she would drown and never see her mother again!

Now each morning Carol and I helped Miss Chew. Miss Chew now had four clothespins ready at her command. I watched with anticipation at Miss Chew's placid face, hoping she'd take the clothespin from me. I looked at Carol's earnest little face and knew the next time it would be her turn. She was pleased there was no favoritism. Although sometimes Miss Chew would forget to take clothespins from one of us twice, we never said a word. Sometimes I knew Miss Chew wanted to laugh at our childish eagerness.

After work Carol and I gleefully ran off to the playground where we'd play all morning. The large playground with all its play equipment had one lone teeter-totter. There used to be two, but (as I told Carol) one time Edna had jumped up and stood in the middle of the board and yelled, "Come on, let's see how many of you can balance me."

We clambered aboard, Edna with outstretched arms balanced precariously. At that moment Miss Reber happened by and we shrieked proudly, "Look at us Miss

Reber!" She smiled and continued on her way.

Suddenly we heard a creaking and then a sharp crack; the teeter-totter was splitting! A nimble Edna jumped down just in time, while the rest of us spilled off.

Laughing hysterically we observed the damage, not realizing Miss Hayes wouldn't think it was funny.

And sure enough, we were in trouble.

Facing us, she implored, "How did the board break?" No one answered.

"It can't break by itself, can it?" she asked.

"No," we replied, as we cowered behind each other.

She then methodically asked each girl if they had been on the board. After everyone who had participated answered, "Yes," she exclaimed, "So that's how the board broke."

And by then we realized in all innocence that Miss Hayes was correct! Exasperated, she told us, "There would be no more standing up on the teeter-totter and only two people allowed on each end. She concluded, "Your punishment is that the broken board will not be replaced."

Now Carol and I looked at the lone board but we knew we were too small and lightweight for this giant teeter-totter, so that morning we decided to play house in the old weathered barns, which once housed farm animals.

There was a deep watering trough near the smaller animal stalls. High above the cement trough was a curved faucet. Our imaginations turned the stalls into our house. The stalls were made of wood which had weathered to a color of grey with flecks of chipped white paint which looked unsightly. We each had a stall which we called our room. The stalls were always dusty and we worked diligently cleaning our imaginary rooms, even though they never quite became clean. Frustrated, we looked around and spied the faucet. With renewed energy we rushed towards the faucet, but it was so high, we could barely twist it. The water trickled down slowly and barely covered the bottom trough. Looking into the deep trough, we could see the water, but couldn't reach it. Straddling one leg over and bending down to get our rags damp, we fell in. Startled and wet, we looked at each other in surprise! Too late, we knew we were in trouble. For an instant, we were scared Miss Chew would be mad at us, although we quickly forgot and played on. We'd dip our rags inthe trough and then go clean our house. Running back and forth, we lost ourselves in our scrubbing and hard work. We worked like beavers, scrubbing up and down with water dripping all over our overalls. With voices full of pride, we'd yell, "Look how clean my house is!" Our faces beamed as we surveyed our clean house.

Then came Miss Reber's call. "Nona, Carol, time for lunch!" Uh oh! We were still wet. We raced outside and stood facing the sun. I patted the front of my overalls, hoping they'd dry faster. With our faces toward the bright sun, eyes closed, we patted faster and harder.

"Carol, is yours getting dryer?" I asked. "No," came her reply.

Then we heard Miss Reber's second call, "Carol, Nona, where are you? It's time for lunch." We stared down at our shoes, darkened with water stains and walked slowly towards the main house, kicking clumps of dirt off our shoes along the way. We walked like snails, hoping each step would dry us.

Bedraggled, we entered the dining room and discovered the teachers were already eating! Miss Chew looked over at us and asked, "You're late! Why?"

Stammering, we both replied, "We got wet while we were playing and wanted to dry ourselves."

"How did you get wet?"

We hung our heads and because I was the oldest I told them, "We were playing house and had to clean our house."

This must have amused the teachers because we were not punished. I could see the teachers holding back their smiles. One had her napkin covering her mouth, stifling a laugh.

Even though they did not appear to be upset, I was still scared. We were then severely scolded and we knew we would never do it again.

Miss Chew had to change our clothes and clean our shoes. I felt awful, she worked so hard. She quickly dressed us and looked at us with a stern face. Carol and I silently exchanged looks. All fresh and clean, with solemn eyes turned toward Miss Chew we both echoed, "Thank you Miss Chew."

Even after this episode, I knew the teachers were relieved I finally had a playmate; and I was glad because Carol and I soon became best friends.

The next day after "work" Carol and I decided to play on the swings when we noticed our gardener near the watering trough.

"Let's go see what he's doing," I cried. "Okay," yelled Carol.

Running to the trough we could see the gardener twisting the faucet off with a wrench.

"What are you doing?" we asked. He looked at us and shrugged.

"Uh-oh!" we looked at each other sheepishly — we knew!

Chapter 7

The Wizened Gardener

laughing, he tortured
with vengeance in mind he killed
karma awaits him

One day just before dinner, Carol and I were in the front of the main house waiting for the first dinner bell to ring signifying it was time to wash up for dinner. Everything was quiet and serene as the late afternoon sun dipped behind the tall pine trees casting elongated shadows before us. Carol and I became impatient waiting for the bell, so we decided to take a chance and stroll on down to the playground. Watching our distorted shadows we pranced and jumped around as our weird shapes mimicked us. Delighted with our silhouettes we approached the playground laughing.

At a distance we saw our wizened gardener outlined against the glow of the sinking sun. Against the orange haze his wispy grey hair appeared to stand straight up like an electrified halo! He looked odd. I wondered why he was still here, as he usually left in the early afternoon. We were told many times not to bother the gardener when he was working but we continued on in his direction. The gardener was leaning against a half broken barn wood fence. His head was bent down and he was holding a pitchfork in front of him and he appeared to be laughing. Coming closer, we saw a tiny bleeding animal stuck through one prong, its brown fur partially matted with blood. We stiffened and asked, "Oooh, what is it?"

"A gopher," the gardener sneered in between his cracklings. My terrified eyes were as big as saucers. I noticed the gopher's eyes were closed in agony and his

two front paws clung
    to the pitchfork.

"But what happened?" we cried in unison. "Why did you do it? Why did you stab it?"

"Because he deserved it," he said, as he twisted the fork deeper into the small creature. He laughed louder as we gasped in terror.

The dying gopher wrenched again as blood oozed from its wound. Once more the gopher's frantic paws were trying in vain to loosen the prong.

"Oooh," I cried in horror while looking at the mean gardener's face. His face was twisted in a sardonic smile. He was enjoying the gopher's frenzied movements.

We ran from the scene as fast as we could. With pounding hearts we raced up from the playground towards the front yard. We sighed with relief at the sight of a teacher. Running up to the teacher with tears blinding our eyes, we hysterically explained what we had just seen. Stumbling over our words we gasped and started over again.

The stone faced teacher listened in disbelief. She questioned us again and again. "Did he just stand there and laugh? Did he stab the gopher again?"

"Yes, yes!" we said catching our breath as salty tears streamed down our faces and dripped on our sunsuits. Wiping our tears with our smudgy hands we asked the teacher, "Why is he so mean? How could he do that to the little gopher?"

She looked at us for a moment and told us, "It's almost time for the first bell to ring, go inside and get cleaned up and be sure to wash your faces!"

. We walked to the bathroom in silence. I wondered why the teacher didn't answer our questions. Using the toilet and washing our grubby hands, we remembered our faces. Splashing the cool water on our faces, we felt a little better. As we were leaving the bathroom, the brass warning bell was being hand rung loudly by an older girl who was on kitchen duty. We quietly waited in the playroom for the girls to come. Like a horde of baby elephants the pounding of running feet was heard above us. There was only 15 minutes to get ready for dinner. We watched them rush past us to the end of the room and put their various toys they had been playing with into their own little cubby holes. Then they hurried to wait their turn to use the bathroom. As the line formed Carol and I were glad we had finished washing up first tonight. We were the first ones to use the clean rolled down towel which by now would be completely wet and turning grey! But the best part, I thought with relief, was getting there early so I didn't have to sit on a damp toilet!

A week went by and then two weeks. The gardener never came. I finally asked the teacher, "Where's the gardener?"

She replied, "The gardener doesn't work here anymore!"

"Oh!" I looked at her in surprise. "Forever?" I asked.

"I don't know," the teacher answered, "but Miss Hayes is looking for another gardener!"

"Uh-oh," I thought the gardener was being punished. Then again, he was really mean! I felt sad again for the little gopher. And yet I felt sorry for the gardener as he had worked hard all day in the scorching sun tending to our different gardens. I realized the gopher had been destructive in the flower beds but what if it had ruined our entire garden? There would be no flowers to admire and smell, and probably the gardener would be in trouble that way also. The poor gardener, he tried to do his best.

Maybe after the flowers died Miss Hayes would think it over and ask him to come back. If only he hadn't laughed so hard or tortured the little creature in front of us, then he'd still have a job. And if we hadn't told on him, then everyone would be happy, everyone but the poor little gopher, of course!

I wondered if it went to heaven.

Chapter 8

County Hospital

I want to go home
no one left to hear my cry
heart aches more than chest

Late one night when I was still a preschooler, I tossed and turned in bed. I felt terrible, my head throbbed, my body was hot and my chest ached from coughing. I tried to get up but was too weak. I cried out in pain, "Miss Chew, I'm sick. I don't feel well." There was no answer. Coughing again I sputtered, "Miss Chew I'm sick."

Miss Chew's bedroom light went on and dim light poured into the Nursery's porch through her adjoining curtained French door.

The door opened swiftly, "Who's sick?" her urgent voice whispered.

"I am, Miss Chew."

She knelt down and felt my feverish head and straightened up quickly. "I'll be right back." She flew downstairs and in a flash was back with Miss Reber. With a flashlight, they looked down my coughing throat. They muttered to each other and I heard the words, "Hurry, I'll go get the car."

Miss Chew wrapped me quickly in a warm blanket and carried me down the front stairs where Miss Reber waited in the car with the motor running. They left in such haste they never stopped to change their pajamas or bathrobes!

Cradled limply in Miss Chew's arms I felt the car speed off into the black night. Miss Reber drove faster than usual. No one spoke but occasionally Miss Reber would ask, "How is she?" Though half dazed, I heard

Miss Chew answer, "She's asleep."

Suddenly Miss Reber saw a flashing light in her mirror, and whispered to Miss Chew, "A policeman!" She slowly eased onto the shoulder.

"Why are you speeding?" the officer questioned.

"We have a sick child," she answered. The officer shined his flashlight in my direction, motioned and said, "Go."

Miss Reber and Miss Chew mumbled under their breath but I could not hear their words.

I stirred and could see the tops of the big trees silhouetted against the car's headlights as they whizzed by one after another. It seemed we should have been downtown at Dr. Harder's office by now, for he was the Home's doctor and was the most gentle man I knew. But Miss Reber continued driving further. I caught a glimpse of Miss Chew's profile as she stared out the car window. I could tell by the expression on her face that I was really sick.

Muted voices woke me. White forms hovered over me. I could not see Miss Reber or Miss Chew and I began to cry.

"Miss Chew! Miss Reber!" I pleaded. But there was no answer from them. I looked at the strangers' faces and cowered and realized I was not in Dr. Harder's office.

One lady in white bent down and said, "I am your nurse, you are in a hospital and I will take care of you."

I looked at them and agonized, "Miss Chew, Miss Reber."

"Sshh, sshh," she shushed, "Miss Chew and Miss Reber had to go home."

Hot tears welled and fell like rain and with both arms outstretched I tried to sit up. I cried out in terror, "I want Miss Reber and Miss Chew! I want to go home too!" But I couldn't. I had been coughing up blood! I had tuberculosis.

Exhausted, I laid back and thought of Miss Chew and

Miss Reber and how they had left me. Once again my whole world was upside down. My mother was gone and now Miss Chew and Miss Reber had left me. I thought of all the girls and I cried and cried until I could cry no more. I stared at the doctors and nurses and would not talk.

When Miss Chew and Miss Reber came to visit me, they couldn't come in the room. They had to stay behind a glass partition because I was contagious. I was glad they were there, but I didn't want to talk to them. I felt too sad. As usual Miss Reber was smiling and she told me everyone said, "Hello." I looked blankly at her. She tried to cheer me up by telling me that Edith (her niece) was going to visit her at the Home again. She knew I liked Edith because she taught us different songs.

Precocious Edith was almost 7 years old and she wore thick glasses which seemed to emphasize her crossed eyes. She was bold and a little overwhelming. She wanted to play with us so she asked us if we knew the 1-2-3 song. "No," we answered. So in her brash voice she proceeded to sing, "1-2-3 / the devil's after me / 4-5-6 / he's up to all his tricks / 7-8-9 / he'll miss me all the time / for I trust in the Lord." When she was through our mouths gaped with amazement. We couldn't believe what we had heard, singing about the devil. The songs we sang never mentioned the devil! Once Miss Reber happened by and heard us singing. She called Edith over and told her not to teach us songs like that anymore! So Edith taught us another song. "Oh Johnny Come Back / oh Johnny Come Back / oh how could you be so mean? / all the neighbor's cats and dogs will never more be seen / all the neighbor's cats and dogs will never be seen / they're all ground up in sausages in Johnny Come Back's machine!"

Incredulously, I gasped, "They're all dead?" "No," Edith shrilled, "it's just a song."

.　　　.　　　.

I looked at Miss Reber's animated face and I was silent.

Miss Chew chimed in, "Hurry and get well Nona, soon the big parade for Pioneer Days will be here and you and Paula will be my little boys again." Miss Chew knew I liked being in the big parade where once a year all the town's people gathered in western garb and all the girls from the Home dressed in exquisite Chinese embroidered outfits, while some wore fancy headpieces.

Paula & Miss Chew

Every year we won ribbons. Paula and I dressed in black boys trousers and shiny black embroidered tops and we donned the traditional round silk hats, which symbolized wisdom. With our moon shaped faces and hats, Miss Chew thought we looked cute and a little wise. We felt special because we were the only Nursery girls dressed like boys, though I secretly yearned for the colorful silk outfits.

Paula, Beverly's younger sister, had huge jet black eyes, was mischievous and always seemed to be in some kind of trouble with Miss Chew. Paula and I always held one end of the long Ming Quong banner and the other Nursery girls marched between us and held the banner also. Following behind us were the older girls, some dressed in ornate Chinese opera outfits. Pansy, the oldest sister of Edna and Nora, dressed differently, wearing a coolie hat and a somber peasant outfit. She was a

Pansy – the vegetable vendor

vegetable vendor with two large baskets of vegetables attached to each end of her long bamboo pole which was slung over one shoulder. With her authentic appearance she dramatized her role and walked bent over with a gait. Her presence always captured the show with loud clapping from the spectators. A newspaper photographer would run in front of us to take our pictures. Marching to the sounds of the Los Gatos High School band filled us with pride.

I looked at Miss Chew's hopeful face but said nothing. Miss Chew and Miss Reber looked at each other with a helpless expression.

But then Miss Reber's face brightened and she said, "When we come back, it will be close to Christmas, so we'll bring you an early Christmas gift."

Miss Reber's comment about Christmas made me even sadder for that meant I would also miss Thanksgiving. And then I wondered how long I had been at the hospital and wondered if I had missed Easter also. All these wonderful holidays with things to do and see.

I thought about Easter and how our church was always gloriously alive. It started with Palm Sunday, when both sides of the middle aisle were decorated with long slender palm leaves. The arching leaves created a scripture scene as pictured in the Bible. And when the minister read about Jesus on the donkey, I could visualize a humble Jesus robed in white riding in victoriously on a docile grey donkey right in the middle of church!

And when Easter Sunday arrived the church was breathtakingly bathed in an abundance of pure-white Easter lilies. Miss Reber always missed this resurrection service, as she was home painstakingly deboning and dicing chicken for our midday Easter dinner. Miss Reber knew we looked forward to this dish of creamy chicken with tender peas and diced carrots which was served only on Easter.

My mind continued to drift to the upcoming holiday, Thanksgiving, when once again Miss Reber's turkey dinner was prepared with care. She took extra time to make sure her mashed potatoes were lump-free, as she knew we appreciated this gesture. Traditional turkey for us meant delicious slivers of turkey with rich brown gravy. We didn't like the bread stuffing and cranberry but the teachers enjoyed them. Our favorite item was the demi-size paper cups filled with gourmet nuts. Sometimes we'd ask permission to save a few for our "annual walk" after our early meal.

This part of Thanksgiving was the most fun. We bundled up against the crisp November air and were divided into groups with an older girl in charge. During these invigorating walks we were permitted to go beyond the Sawyer's house and even further up the steep hill past another neighbor's Spanish home (which overlooked our Home). The Stillwell's c-shaped hacienda had an open courtyard with century plants and giant cactuses.

"Oooh," we'd marvel, "Look at the Stillwell's house, isn't it pretty?"

The Stillwells had a curly-haired daughter named Natalie who was in my Sunday School class. Her Sunday outfits were sometimes dreamy white organza dresses with patent-leather shoes and stockings trimmed with lace. I thought she was so lucky, and to live in such a beautiful unusual house.

Natalie had an older good-looking brother, who one time remarked to his friends, that at night he could look right into the Home's cottage. When the Cottage girls heard that terrible truth, they shrieked in terror, "Did he see us getting undressed." After that the girls undressed in the dark or under the bed covers (the cottage had no curtains).

And then after the Stillwell's house we were faced with unfamiliar paths splitting off in different directions, each way offered exciting discoveries.

Once we passed a beautiful Chinese-style house, painted an unusual dungeon grey. It looked austere nestled under the tall dark trees and surrounded by a high foreboding black-wrought iron gate. Brass fixtures adorned the gate and the front door. We always wondered who lived there. The silence and darkness surrounding the house was foreboding, yet reverent at the same time.

Coming down the hill we took another turn and off to the side was an old white framed house with its side door ajar. We were surprised there was no sound of anyone around. So a few older girls ventured forth while the younger ones followed. We saw a dinette set in the middle of the kitchen area with dishes and utensils. On the counter were pots and pans strewn about. We looked at each other and someone whispered, "Ghosts!" We ran from the deserted house certain that the ghosts were behind us!

We told our nurse about this house, she looked serious and said, "Do not go to that house again. Most of these houses are summer homes."

We didn't know what a summer home meant, but we avoided the house. But sometime later, taking another path, we unexpectedly passed the house again and this time the front door was open. From the road we could see that many household items were missing. This time we believed that this was indeed a haunted house and off we ran, with our screams echoing throughout the hill-side.

We never told the teachers what we saw the second time, as we knew our punishment would probably be no more walks.

.   .   .

Now as the days passed I grew stronger. Miss Chew and Miss Reber visited again. This time I could sit in a chair in a special glass enclosed room. Outside this enclosure the other hospitalized children played. I watched Miss Reber approach carrying a long narrow brown box. As they stopped at my glassed area they handed the box to my nurse. I looked at it solemnly. Miss Reber and Miss Chew's expectant faces waited for me to open the box, but I just stared at them. Finally with much coaxing I lifted the lid. Inside was a huge doll with brown curly hair. Although her eyes were closed, I noticed she had unusually long eyelashes. She was outfitted with a blue organdy dress with tiny polka dots. The hem was edged with a white ruffle.

Miss Reber said cheerfully, "Lift it up." I did and her eyes opened. I looked up at Miss Reber and gazed back down at my first doll, and I still could not smile or even say thank you. The Christmas season was near and my body ached with loneliness. All I wanted was to go home.

As I got better, another patient about 7 years old would sneak into my room constantly when the nurses weren't around. She talked a lot about Christmas and what she wanted to receive. She showed me her hand puppet and I showed her my new doll; she was speechless, it seemed she had never seen anything so beautiful and I could sense she wanted one like mine. Pretty soon I got used to her visits, and I would just lie there and listen to her talk silly things through her little puppet; slowly I responded and soon she had me laughing.

After a while the girl got well and went home. I didn't know it could be so quiet. I missed her and her incessant chattering.

Christmas trees twinkled merrily in the visiting room brightening the sterile hospital. I wished the other girl could have seen the pretty decorations. I wondered if she would get a doll for Christmas, but I didn't think she would because her family looked so poor.

I thought of the girls and teachers at home preparing for Christmas, decorating a freshly cut tree with strings of colored lights, old-fashioned ornaments and my favorite decoration, the freshly strung popcorn, because we could always sneak a few bites.

The other ritual I loved was watching the teachers set up the manger scene with each delicate porcelain figurine carefully positioned inside a built-in sitting bench. When each figure was in place we huddled down eagerly in anticipation for the spotlight to be turned on. And when that happened, it was magic; everything seemed to come alive. We were transformed to that holy night in Bethlehem and we'd whisper, "Look at baby Jesus."

Even during the day when the light was off, I'd tip-toe respectfully by so I could peek at baby Jesus lying in the manger wrapped in swaddling clothes.

For Christmas we usually received practical gifts like toothpaste and hand-knitted gloves from church members. Sometimes we opened gifts of fruit like a giant orange and always some type of toy, like jacks or a jump rope. But one year it was extra special. When the movie show "Snow White and the Seven Dwarfs" played at the only theater in town, my group of seven Nursery girls received a dwarf soap. And a surprised Miss Chew was given a Snow White soap. My soap was Dopey, because I was the youngest. I loved Dopey's charming smile and slouchy purple hat.

We cherished and played with our soap as long as we could until we had to give them up because Miss Chew needed them for our baths. How I wished Miss Chew would stop lathering our hair and scrubbing us so hard. She didn't seem to care as the soap faded, got smaller and lost its shape.

On Christmas Eve, we sang Christmas hymns and later snuggled in bed while we listened to the older girls caroling outside.

Homesickness welled up in me and I sobbed under my covers. Clutching my new doll I finally fell asleep.

.   .   .

Soon Miss Reber and Miss Chew came to the hospital for the last time. They brought my clothes, I was going home! I was overjoyed.

On the way home I wrapped my arms around my doll so tightly Miss Reber turned and laughingly said, "Be careful Nona."

Looking at Miss Chew and Miss Reber I cheerfully said, "I'm taking my doll home." I knew nothing could hurt me now.

"What is your doll's name?" Miss Reber asked.

"Dolly," I answered brightly. That night, I snuggled close to Dolly.

"Good night, Miss Chew."

"Good night, Nona." Then she saw Dolly and chided

me, "You can't sleep with Dolly."

"Why?" I asked, surprised.

"Because you'll play with her and never fall asleep." "But..." Miss Chew didn't listen to me. She took Dolly out of my warm bed and placed her on my chair at the foot of the bed. Although I was happy to be home, I felt dejected and also felt sorry for Dolly as she was all alone.

After breakfast the next morning, I fixed my bed and smoothed out the wrinkles in my bedspread. Miss Chew placed Dolly at the head of the bed.

"Miss Chew I want to play with Dolly."

"No, you might get her dirty." Woefully, I looked at Miss Chew as she continued, "She looks nice there and when we have visitors they'll be able to see your doll all neat and pretty."

I looked at Miss Chew and thought to myself, I wouldn't get her dirty. Leaving the bedroom porch, I turned and looked at Dolly with her bright eyes and sweet smile. She did look nice and pretty on my bed.

"Bye, Dolly," I said softly, "I have to help Miss Chew with the wash and then I'm going grocery shopping with Miss Reber." Later that day, as I was looking out the window of the car, my body tensed as Miss Reber stopped at the intersection of Loma Alta and High streets. A left turn would take us downtown, and a right turn would take us to the San Jose County Hospital.

"Miss Reber, which way are you going?" I cried.

"Why Nona, we're going downtown," she answered as she turned left.

Relief ran through my tense body as I replied, "I don't want to go to the hospital again."

After that episode, Miss Reber continued to play her game with me. Whenever we approached that intersection she'd ask, "Which way do you want to go, Nona?"

She chuckled when I answered, "left."

One time Miss Chew was in the car and Miss Reber nudged her and asked the same question and I replied, "left." They were amused. I was too scared to say anything and felt so relieved when she turned left, that I forgot their teasing. I sat back joyfully and looked out the crystal clear windows of the car. The whole world looked brighter.

Chapter 9

Saving Face

face to face, I see
same flesh of flesh, blood of blood
yet — so far apart

One warm afternoon, when I was around 6 years old, I was out in the front yard talking to my friends when Mrs. Lee, who was across the way under the shade of my beloved pepper tree called over to me, "Nona, please come here." I walked over and noticed a new girl, who was partially obscured by the lacy branches of the tree. She was standing next to Mrs. Lee studying me.

I wondered who she was, as no one had mentioned anything about a new girl arriving. But I could see that this girl was older and that was probably why us younger girls had not heard of her coming.

I then wondered why Mrs. Lee just called me over and not my friends also. As I approached Mrs. Lee I sensed an air of excitement all around her. Her face glowed and her eyes sparkled. Mrs. Lee's excited voice emphasized her Chinese accent as she twittered in a sing-song fashion, "Aah, Nu-naa, I have good news for you."

"Good news?" I repeated.

"Yes, Nu-naa, very good news."

Mrs. Lee placed her hand upon the girl's shoulder and beamed, "Nu-naa, this new girl is your sister!"

"My sister?" I gasped.

"Yes, Nu-naa, isn't that nice?"

But I could not respond (as my mind became blank!) What Mrs. Lee was saying was unbelievable! For I never ever in my whole life thought I had a sister.

I focused in on Mrs. Lee's face to make sure what I

had just heard was the truth for even though I didn't doubt her, it was just too much to understand.

Mrs. Lee continued, "Nu-naa, your sister's name is Emma, and you know Nu-naa she said joyously, she will live here at Ming Quong with us also and she will be in my Lok-Hin group."

"Isn't that nice, Nu-naa you have a sister? Nu-naa?"

"Yes," I answered timidly and that was all I could say. I felt too shy in front of my sister.

I looked at my sister expectantly, but there was no response. She was aloof. Puzzled by my sister's attitude, I became a little frightened; she didn't seem nice at all. I wondered why. Maybe she was shy too or maybe she was even scared. For I remembered my first day at the Home and how scared I had been. It made me sad again to recall how I had screamed and cried and thought my whole world had ended. I still wondered about my mother, maybe she'll come to the Home next, maybe she'll want me back again. I missed my mother. I missed her very much. I stared at this girl, my sister, and wondered what she was thinking. If she felt like crying or had any fears, they were well hidden. Maybe by instinct she was acting out the old Chinese saying, "saving face," keeping all her emotions within her and acting like nothing bothered her. I then wondered if she even liked me because it seemed she didn't. Many questions began to swirl in my mind. Who had brought her to the Home?

Was it a relative or was it a stranger?

Did she, like me, miss whomever she had lived with?

Had she been abandoned also?

I wondered where she had lived and did she know our mother?

Were there any more of us?

But as the days passed all these questions were left behind for what I thought would be happy days with my sister turned out to be disappointing days. My sister and I did not play and walk and talk and laugh together as most of the other sisters at the Home did. I guess because she was seven years older than me, she didn't want to pal around with a little Nursery girl! But no matter what the reason was I was just satisfied with the knowledge that I had a sister. That was going to have to be enough; it was all she would give.

But there were times when my sister and I were drawn together because we did have one common trait — our bad eating habits!

We both ate slowly. In fact we ate so slowly that after the rest of the household was finished, Emma and I had to take our food outside behind the barn to finish eating there. We were kept apart from each other so we wouldn't talk, which of course was unnecessary! Not only were we now out of the teacher's way where they couldn't see us, but we were in plain view of the girls who could see these two naughty girls being punished!

I couldn't truly understand why we were punished for eating slow, for though I tried to eat quickly, I just couldn't.

But another form of punishment which I think was worse, was the use of a white folded bonnet. When this bonnet was opened and placed over the girl's head, it shielded her face completely and she resembled the old Dutch cleanser container, "the girl with no face." As the teachers surmised this kept the "slow-poke" eaters eyes from roving and the result would be a faster eater. It worked, but the poor girl's self-esteem was as low as the last man on the totem pole; no one could talk to the "bad girl." This situation created such an awkward atmosphere at the table that no one ever felt like talking anyway!

This innocent-looking bonnet which Miss Hayes once used for gardening was also used for anyone who talked too much, whether at the dining table or some other function where a girl had been out of line. And once the guilty girl arrived at the dining table she would see that this form of punishment was to be used, as the bonnet was at her designated place. The head of the Home would then announce that we were to ignore her, so she would learn her lesson.

Punishments like these and many others bonded the girls closer as we always agreed, "the teachers were so mean!"

For me, mush at the Home was my worst enemy! Oh how I dreaded this tasteless gruel. On one particular school morning the mush had so many lumps I couldn't swallow my mouthful. The girls at my table urged, "Hurry, Nona, finish your mush."

But I couldn't. A lump that felt like the size of a golf ball was stuck in my throat. I stared silently at my bowl of mush. The teacher at my table was silent, as all the girls finished their breakfast and excused themselves.

Breakfast this morning was fruit, toast, mush, hot chocolate and our usual cup of hot water to prevent constipation. I was left alone in the dining room; even Emma had finished her mush and was gone. Desperately, I watched the two girls on dining room duty clear and wash the tables. The girl assigned to clean my table asked me to move and so I moved to another dirty table. Soon the girls would sweep the floor and I'd be completely alone. As I lifted the spoon to my mouth I felt my stomach turn. Teary eyed, I looked at the older girls and one girl advised, "Just put it in your mouth, Nona, and swallow it fast and don't taste it." I felt so queasy, I couldn't even answer her.

Miss Reber came in to inspect the dining room and said, "Nona, you haven't finished your mush yet! I guess you'll have to take it out to the playroom."

I headed towards the dark playroom. I knew all the girls were doing their morning chores and getting ready for school. Anxiety filled my body; I did not want to be late for school.

I stiffened as I heard the sound of Miss Bankes' heavy missionary style shoes thunder in the hushed playroom. She looked down at my bowl of cold mush and snapped,

"Are you going to finish your mush?"

I noticed through her rimmed glasses, the one eye that was always half shut was twitching rapidly; it had an eerie glint to it. It looked like a pirate's eye without the patch. I started to shudder.

"Nona, what's the matter with you?"

I almost cried. I quivered, "I can't because I'll throw up!"

"Shame on you Nona," she spat out angrily and with her finger she brushed her cheek repeatedly to shame me. "Don't you know there are hundreds of hungry children in this world who have nothing to eat?"

I shook my head and looked at her soulfully.

With exasperation, Miss Bankes hissed, "You're being naughty Nona. Do you want to be punished?"

Looking down at my bowl I answered, "No, please," and shook my head.

"Well, you are going to be late for school. Do you want to be late for school?"

Again, I emphatically nodded, "No."

"Well then eat your mush!"

I looked down at my mush, which by now had formed into a hard solid mass as a tear trickled down my cheek.

With a shrug of her shoulder, Miss Bankes let out an exasperated sound. "Get up right now!" Get your chores done and get ready for school. I'll give your mush to Miss Reber and she'll save it for your dinner!"

I rushed upstairs to the Nursery room and quickly fixed my bed. Next I got out the dust rag and hastily dusted off the dressers and chairs.

I stopped for I had to go to the bathroom. After I was done I yelled, "Miss Chew I'm through!"

Miss Chew hurried out of her bedroom and exclaimed, "Nona, you're late!"

"I know Miss Chew," I said. I bent over so she could check my bowel movements. Miss Chew had to check all the Nursery girls' bowel movements. If we didn't do enough, we had to sit until we did. I was glad today, of all days, I did enough.

Miss Chew wiped me quickly and asked, "Did you do your job?"

"Yes," I answered.

"All right Nona I'll check it and you hurry and get dressed." With a flurry, I brushed my teeth, put on my dress and sweater, combed my hair and grabbed my hanky. I knocked at Miss Chew's bedroom door which was opened and breathlessly called out, "Miss Chew, I'm ready to go to school." With an experienced eye she surveyed my appearance and nodded her approval.

I dashed down to the kitchen for my lunch bag and was almost out the playroom door, when I heard Miss Reber's reminder, "Don't bang the door!"

"I won't," I cried.

I could see the girls ahead of me, but I couldn't catch up with them. I called their names and yelled, "Please wait for me," but they didn't hear me. I ran as fast as I could. Tears ran down my face. As I approached the school, I heard the school bell ringing. I bounded into my first grade classroom and everyone was already seated. The teacher's eyes followed me to my seat but she didn't say a word. I quickly went to the back of the cloak room and put my brown paper lunch bag on the shelf and hung my sweater on my hook. Hastily, I sat down at my desk.

No one paid any attention to me or asked me why I was late. It was as if I wasn't late. I felt relieved and wiped the perspiration from my face with my zig zag hanky. I felt a little better. Hurriedly, I put my hanky away. I didn't want anyone to see those old stains which were now embedded in the fabric. How I yearned to have a pure white embroidered lace handkerchief like my classmates. Once I found a hanky edged with lace on the cloakroom floor and I quickly put it in the pocket of my red coat. The teacher who was a substitute noticed it and held it up with all the items from my pocket in front of the entire classroom and asked, "Who owns these?" I reluctantly raised my hand. I was so humiliated and scared, as the teacher reproached me to turn the hanky into the lost and found box next time because it is the right thing to do.

And now as this teacher called the roll she called out, "Nona..."

"Here!" I quaked. She looked at me knowingly and kindly overlooked my tardiness. This time I felt I had the kindest teacher in all the school, for I felt she knew that girls from Ming Quong were conscientious.

During recess time I strolled around the grounds and stopped to watch my favorite game of tetherball. The older girl, on dining room duty from the Home, sidled over and asked, "Were you late?"

"Yeah," I replied.

"What did the teacher say?" "Nothing."

"Really? You're lucky she didn't send you to Mr. Fisher's office."

"Yeah, I'm glad," I answered with relief, "I would be scared to go to the principal's office."

The girl continued, "What did Miss Bankes do?"

Nona – 3rd row left.
Nora – 2nd row – 3rd. Beverly – 3rd - right

"She scolded me and she saved my mush for dinner."

"Oooh, she's really mean. At least she's not going to put a diaper on you and call you a baby."

"Oh, I know, that's the worst punishment yet. Miss Bankes was so mean to my sister, but she didn't even say anything to me about a diaper!"

I was grateful for that as I remembered one time when Emma could not finish her mush. Miss Bankes had put a diaper over her play clothes and made her go outside to the playground. Whispers of, "Look at her! She's being punished because she didn't finish her mush." When I saw her, I was speechless. I was horrified. I could not believe Miss Bankes could be so cruel. As my sister climbed the first step of the iron bars she turned and looked in our direction, and I saw her agonized eyes. I felt empathy for her. No one spoke, they just stared. Emma's face was mirrored in pain and her grief was devastating. I couldn't bear to look at her. I turned my head and ran as fast as I could to the ding-dong bell. The gazebo offered a private sanctuary to retreat from her misery and suffering eyes. I didn't want to be a part of the girls who might be whispering about her and worst of call, calling her a "big baby."

The school bell rang and recess was over. Walking back to our classrooms, I asked the older girl, "I wonder why Miss Bankes didn't punish me that way?"

"Because," she answered seriously, "Your sister is older. She is different from you. She's stand offish and has a real stubborn streak!"

"Oh," I answered understandingly, "but I still think it's mean."

"So do I," shrugged the older girl.

She continued, "Do you like your sister?"

"I guess so, but I never play with her or anything, I just see her walking by with the older girls."

The older girl continued, "Remember the picture Miss Reber took of you and Emma?"

"What picture?" I asked.

"The one of you two on the big flat rock. In that picture she looks like she likes you."

"Oh yeah, I remember. Miss Reber told Emma to put her arm around me and when she did, it made us laugh."

The girl paused and looked at me and said, "You two look like sisters, but you're opposites — you're fun and she isn't."

Nona and Emma

I looked at her and was a little embarrassed. "That's true," she stated.

As we parted, I solemnly waved good-bye. I thought about what she said, and I felt an emptiness. But although I felt left out, I could at least brag to the younger girls, "I've got a sister!" Yet when I had done that, I had felt funny, for I knew that the girls who had befriended me when I first came to the Home, that they and my other new friends were truly my bonded sisters, and that Emma, who was a stranger to me, was my sister only because Mrs. Lee had told me so.

Emma at the Ding-Dong Bell

Chapter 10

Caged

teacher's wrath explodes
losing sight of God within
mars child deeply

It was always a day to look forward to when a new girl arrived at the Home, especially if she was to be in your age group. And if she was, we wondered what she'd be like. Would she be nice, fun and easy to get along with or what?

I remembered when Harlan, who was a year younger than me arrived from Minneapolis, Minnesota. As we gathered around her, we questioned her about Minneapolis, as none of us had ever heard of such a place.

Harlan replied, "Minneapolis is far, far away and very different from California. In fact she emphasized, "You wouldn't like it there."

"Why?" we asked.

"Because it's real cold there and it snows a lot."

"Snow!" we clamored. We were impressed, as it never really snowed in Los Gatos. But snowflakes had drifted down twice, but had melted right before our eyes, so to hear first hand about playing or walking in the snow was exciting. But Harlan couldn't care less.

I was fascinated with any stories Harlan could tell. One day while chatting with her, she showed me a small folded brochure which she had brought with her to the Home. This pamphlet was all about life at the Ming Quong orphanage. This surprised and intrigued me. Why, I thought was this brochure written about us? Maybe we were important to somebody!

It was a rich-looking brochure with its glossy white

and red paper. It told about the idyllic atmosphere of the Home. It contained several photographs, one of the girls working in the kitchen and the other picture showed apricots drying on trays in the field, which had been cut by the older girls. I was so fascinated by this brochure that I begged Harlan for it. But she said, "No." I persevered and never gave up. Finally months later she relented. I couldn't believe it was mine; as Harlan was famous for not giving into anything or anyone. In fact, it was for that reason her nickname was, "Heartless!"

By now the deep folds of the brochure were frayed and some words were indiscernible. Handling it carefully I reread the brochure endlessly. It described how all the Ming Quong girls were cooperative and enjoyed pitching in and helping out at the Home. This part surprised me, as there were always disgruntled girls who disliked their chores, especially the older girls assigned to kitchen duty for a month. They called the kitchen work, "K.P." and just like the army, they too had mountains of potatoes to peel. Some days to lighten their load and to see Miss Reber smile, the girls would sing, "We're in the army now" or "This is the army Mr. Jones." And at the appropriate part of the lyrics, they'd exaggerate the "toot-toot," which had the kitchen rocking with laughter.

Saturdays at the Home meant extra house duties, not only because we were home from school, but because of our religious upbringing.

As the Bible said, "When God created the heavens and the earth he labored for six days and rested on the seventh day." And as we were taught, we also labored, especially on the sixth day.

But we knew of one small grocery store just outside of town that was opened seven days a week. When we told Miss Hayes about this situation and wondered about the man who worked there, she told us that it was wrong and that it was a sin. We were stunned, for now this man was doomed, for surely when he died he would most certainly not go to heaven.

So Saturdays the dining room and kitchen crew had the most work. They scrubbed, mopped floors, cleaned out cupboards, polished tons of silverware and washed the all-white woodwork.

One Saturday Frances, who was on "K.P.", had been vigorously scrubbing the wall and could not get some grease marks off. She knew this wall would never pass inspection.

Miss Reber sympathetically urged, "Try some elbow

grease." A grateful Frances searched the storage cabinet but couldn't find the elbow grease. She called out, "Miss Reber, what does it look like?" Miss Reber smiled!

Each Saturday after breakfast, Miss Chew had the older girls line up with their bottom sheet to be exchanged for a freshly laundered one. For economic reasons we rotated out sheets. But back then we never gave it any thought as to why we did not get two clean sheets.

At one time it was part of Miss Chew's duty to wash the sheets, but soon it became too much of a burden with her full schedule. The sheets were then contracted out to the Kerful laundry service in town.

This was a positive change for all of us. We loved the scent of the newly starched sheets and it was fun to see who could make the best corners with our crisp sheets.

There has always been one sad incident which stood out in my mind about clean sheets. Alice, a Starlight girl had the unfortunate habit of wetting her bed. When that happened she was forced to drag her mattress down the long flight of stairs outside to the front yard to dry. Loud sobs broke forth from her as tears streamed down her anguished face. The mattress was cumbersome and as she rounded the sharp corners some girls attempted to help her, but they were immediately reprimanded by the teacher. They were told, "You are not permitted to help her for that is her punishment."

In one of the stories we were taught, wasn't someone else punished and made to carry a heavy load also?

Once outside Alice had to raise and tug at her heavy mattress in order to drape it over the fence. It was futile; most of the mattress was on the ground: Alice suffered more humiliation as other girls asked, "Whose mattress was that and why was it out in the front yard?"

It was implied that if Alice had not been so lazy, this would not have happened.

After the second bed-wetting, it then became the teacher's duty to wake Alice up in the middle of the night to use the bathroom.

Laziness was not permitted at the Home, as that was not a good Christian virtue. As a result, Saturday evening we stayed up one hour longer to enable us to groom ourselves for church. We bathed, washed our hair, clipped our fingernails and toenails. and then we polished our dull Buster Brown shoes with Shinola and shined

Ready for Sunday School (hankies in tow!)

According to Luella (in her time) children of inter-racial marriages were banned from entering the Home. But during my time, as is evident by the pictures, the ban was lifted.

them till they looked practically new and reflected our faces. We valued our Buster Brown shoes as it was only given to you when you were in Starlight. These expensive practical- looking shoes were our only shoes, but because of the shoes' reputation for durability, the Home felt it was worth the extra expense. We coveted the prized emblem inside the shoe. But most of all we loved the wooden heels, for when we walked it made wonderful "gok-gok" sounds, which made us feel grown- up and important.

Sunday before we left for the Presbyterian Sunday school and church in town, each group of girls lined up in front of their teacher for extra inspection.

Each girl stepped up with both arms extended towards

the teacher. She checked our nails, and our brushed hair. We then turned around to make sure our slip was not showing beneath our special Sunday dress. She made sure our white socks were folded neatly over just above our shoes. And then the last thing she made sure of was that each girl had their hanky in tow.

As always, everything and everyone at the Home was spotless for that was the sign of good discipline and good Christian upbringing.

.   .   .

About one month later, in the late afternoon, Carol came running to me. She cupped her hands and whispered in my ear, "Have you seen Ida? She's locked in the cage!"

Startled, I gasped, "What cage? The cage in the drying room?" I repeated, "The cage in the drying room?"

"Yes, the one in the corner."

Then I remembered the mesh cage, and uttered in alarm, "Oh, THAT one!" For years I had walked by the cage as I helped Miss Chew with the wash. The cage was always empty and never used, except for the top which the older girls had used to dry their sweaters.

Flabbergasted, I cried, "Why?"

"Someone said she stole a hair barrette and she's being punished."

"Ida stole a barrette?"

"Yes, you should see her!"

"But who told you?"

"An older girl walked by after she finished her ironing and saw her."

I couldn't believe what was happening. How cruel! How mean! How could Miss Hayes do this to Ida, who was always a model girl?

Bewildered, we headed towards the laundry room. Going down a flight of stone stairs we entered the large drying room. The smell of freshly ironed clothes drifted from the adjoining room where three cottage girls were ironing. The room had two windows, but was very dark and cool as it was just below ground level. While our eyes adjusted to the darkness we could make out the oversized cage in the farthest corner of the room. We could see Ida's huddled form; she was hunched forward as the cage was too low for her to sit upright. I noticed that her head appeared distorted. Coming closer, I gasped as Ida's entire head was covered with barrettes. Every inch of her hair was pulled tightly and clasped. It looked like Ida had no hair at all, only barrettes. A dreadful silence surrounded us. Carol and I looked at each other painfully. Our hearts went out for Ida, but we knew we couldn't help her.

I had always liked Ida and thought she was one of the nicest girls at the Home. She was now staring straight ahead past us. Her huge unblinking eyes were solid black with no hues of brown. She did not move, she was so still. She appeared transfixed. We were not permitted to talk to anyone being punished. If caught doing so we would also be punished or now even caged!

Watching Ida staring stoically ahead, we knew instinctively she would not give in to her punishment. Even if her body ached and her legs cramped, she would not lay down to rest no matter how long she was kept in the cage.

While walking away, I could feel Ida's eyes on my back. I felt a terrible sense of helplessness. We could not even say good- bye.

I thought of Miss Hayes' looming figure; coupled with a strange looking hump on her back, she could look even scarier and menacing when she was provoked. Poor Ida.

Miss Hayes' behavior was always puzzling to me. At the dinner table, if any girl slouched, she'd say crossly, "Sit up straight! Do you want a hunchback?" Without a word we'd look at her and straighten up. I always wondered if she forgot she had a hunchback!

Once outside the bright sun made us scowl. As our eyes adjusted to the bright sunlight, I said to Carol, "I feel sad, don't you?"

Carol's solemn face nodded up and down. We headed towards the playground and I continued, "Miss Hayes sure is mean. Since she has been head of the Home she punishes us more."

"Yeah, I know," Carol grumbled.

"Remember Miss Bankes who used to be head of the Home?" "Uh-huh."

"She was mean too, but not that mean!" "Yeah," Carol agreed.

"It seems like when they're new teachers they're real nice. Remember when Miss Hayes first came to the Home and she gave us marshmallows to make into rabbit candies?"

"We were so happy she was the new head of the home, remember?"

"I remember," she answered.

"That was fun," Carol smiled.

"And remember on Halloween she gave us a party?" "Yeah," Carol answered, "the whole playroom was decorated and Miss Hayes was dressed like a scarecrow with a funny looking straw hat and she had on overalls with straw poking out of the pockets."

"Yeah, she made us all laugh. And then we bobbed for apples and played other games."

"And remember why we got that party?"

"Uh-huh, because of a poor baby."

And so that night the party came about because some older girls had asked Miss Hayes if they could "trick or treat" just like their classmates at school had planned to do.

The reply was, "No."

The reason for that answer, as we were told by the older girls, involved a story of a poor, young mother and her baby. On Halloween night some kids dressed in scary costumes rang her door bell and hollered, "Trick or treat." The mother didn't know what to do. She was afraid that if she didn't give them something they would play a trick on her. So she gave them the only thing she had in the house, an orange. And so her poor baby starved.

When we heard that story, we felt so sorry for the baby. We thought Halloween was mean and wondered why the school kids thought trick or treating was fun.

Back then, I didn't even know that the word "treat" usually meant candy!

Now as Carol and I continued to talk about Miss Hayes, I asked Carol, "I wonder why Miss Hayes is so mean?"

No answer, but it didn't matter because it seemed to me that some teachers were just mean and some were real nice and kind.

The sad part was the nice new ones didn't stay long; they always left! That made us sad and resentful as we suspected they didn't approve of Miss Hayes.

I didn't feel right. Even though the day was warm, I felt an icy chill throughout my body. The day was unlike other carefree days. Ida's vacant stare was still etched in my mind. Feeling listless I stopped to sit on a rough cement slab adjacent to the playground. Carol continued on to the playground. Realizing I wasn't following her, she stopped and hollered, "Come on Nona, don't you want to play?"

"No," I called back.

"What are you going to do, just sit there?"

I sighed, "I guess so."

"But why?"

"I don't know. I just feel sad."

Poor Ida. I wondered how long she would be caged. I could still see her hunched over, when suddenly a horrifying thought crossed my mind — would Ida get a hunchback too?

I stood up with a rush and screamed, "Carol!" No answer. Then with all my might, I hollered, "Carol, wait for me, I'm coming, I want to tell you something!"

Catching up with Carol, I told her my thoughts. Carol replied, "I think Ida will be out by dinner time.

Carol was right, and to our relief, Ida did not have a hunchback!

Prior to working at Ming Quong, Miss Hayes was a missionary in Korea, a third world country which often caged offenders and left them in the heart of town to be publicly ridiculed. Did Miss Hayes witness this type of punishment and thought it would be effective for the girls at the Home?

I don't know if anyone ever knew the reason for Miss Hayes' choice of discipline that day, but it is a very sad memory for me and other Ming Quong girls.

As for the memorable Halloween party, that was the only party I recalled at the Home. But some of the girls (after my time) did have a celebration on their birthday with a cake baked specially by Miss Reber. The birthday girl was privileged to choose six girls to sit with her during her birthday dinner.

As a grown up, I felt my birthday was just a day like any other, except for the big ones, starting at age 50, 60, etc.

But now, as I've watched my customers (at my clothing and gift store) celebrate their birthdays by purchasing a special dress or taking the day off from work, I realize their joy and now understand the significance of a birthday.

Chapter 11

Victory Gardens

what does it all mean
flashing the peace sign? — men died
broken families

It was 1941 and the whole world was at war! We listened quietly as Miss Hayes announced after our lunch that World War II was on. I thought war must be really bad, as Miss Hayes and all the teachers looked grave and even the older girls' faces looked so serious. Some looked as though they might even cry!

The hushed dining room was ominously still. Sitting on my stool I looked around and wondered why everyone looked so depressed. I wondered what war meant.

Miss Hayes' serious voice continued, "President Roosevelt of the United States has just broadcast over the radio that he needs everyone in this country to help. The one way we can help the President is to plant victory gardens, and so after lunch there will be no naps!" Now I knew for sure this was serious as naps were always a top priority.

Miss Hayes separated us into two groups, the younger and the older girls with specific vegetables to be planted for each victory garden. And she added, if there was any space left, the older girls could try growing watermelon.

Our faces brightened as we all loved watermelon. I looked over at the next dining table where Beatrice was sitting. She was beaming. I knew she was thinking of her father who always bought watermelons for our Sunday dessert each time he visited her.

Now in between Beatrice's father's visits, we could have our very own melons.

I then looked at Diane, who was at my table. Diane was about four years younger than me. Her father also bought a surprise for all of us on his visits.

I remember one Sunday when Jenny and I were walking home from church when Diane's father who had been waiting for her outside the church drove by with Diane in the front seat. He honked the horn lightly and asked if we wanted a ride home. We were delighted and jumped in the back seat. On the floor of the back seat was a crate of little pink berries. We asked him, "What is this?"

"Raspberries," he replied politely, "Be careful not to step on them."

"We won't," we said as we both bent down to inhale the sweet-smelling berries. Mmmm, mmm, what a tempting fragrance. Without a word we both popped a raspberry in our mouths! My mouth exploded with sweetness. It was heavenly. We could barely contain our happiness.

As we straightened up, I could see Diane's father looking at us through the rear-view mirror. I'm sure our sheepish faces gave us away. But Diane's father who had an air of friendly sophistication about him pretended not to notice. Diane never knew! We would have been so embarrassed as it was Diane's choice to give us a ride home.

I now wondered if we could ask Miss Hayes to let us grow raspberries also. A victory garden could be yummy and fun if it was full of raspberries!

And now after lunch when we were all dismissed from the dining room, I asked an older girl, "What is war."

"That's when men fight," she replied.

"You mean they fight and argue like Nora and Frances?"

"Yes," the older girl continued, "but it's worse because they use guns to shoot and kill each other."

"Guns? You mean they die?"

"Yes."

"But why?" I innocently asked.

"Because they're mean men, Nona, they're Japs!"

I watched the older girl's angry face as she spat out the word, "Jap." I mouthed the word and asked, "What are Japs?"

"Japs are Japanese men, who shoot and kill American men. They are our enemy. They are very bad men, Nona."

As we parted, heading for our separate age groups to start cultivating our gardens, the older girl turned and held up her hand with two fingers spread apart, signaling a V and triumphantly called out to me, "V is for victory Nona, we're going to win the war!"

I was puzzled; what did it all mean?

Once outside we gathered around while Miss Chew with the help of an older girl tilled and dug the soil. The deeper they dug the richer the soil was and that's when I became excited, for they might dig deep enough and end up in China, because that's what the girls had always said.

"Miss Chew," I cried, "are you going to dig to China?" "No, Nona, that's not true," she laughed.

"But some girls said so," I sighed.

Miss Chew made no comment and I thought maybe she was right because we had already tried to dig our way to China and had gotten nowhere! On the playground we dug with little sticks while the rocky hard soil filled with pebbles kept falling back in the hole. We were so disappointed as we thought if we could make it to China, then the people who were very poor could climb up the hole and come live with us and the children could go to school and play with us all day on the playground. That would be fun as there would also be more Chinese people in our town. But now I could see even with the two of them digging there was no sign of China. I sighed, for now I couldn't even ask or watch the gardener dig as he seemed to be gone for good.

Our victory gardens flourished with our home-grown enthusiasm. An abundance of vegetables carpeted our once unused land. At harvest time, joyous sounds rang out when we pulled out the hidden radishes and squiggly-shaped carrots. "Look at mine," or "Look at this funny one," we'd shout. We couldn't believe that these vegetables were once little dots of seeds. Like the gold-mountain men seeking their fortune, our pleasure plus our treasures was pure gold.

But the watermelon patch was a sad sight, although the thick vines produced some funny-looking light-green round melons, these melons never matured or even looked like regular watermelons. Maybe the older girls who were in charge of that patch didn't water regularly!

And we never planted raspberries, for Miss Hayes said they were hard to grow. But, I'm sure if the gardener had been there, he could have worked his magic.

Now at dinner time there was never any left-over vegetables because the home- grown flavor was outstanding. This made Miss Reber happy.

When Miss Hayes used her dessert spoon to ding her water glass, all talking in the room ceased. All heads turned to Miss Hayes' table as she announced which group had grown the prepared vegetables, she praised us for our help and good work and we all beamed with self pride and felt very patriotic.

"Doing this," she continued, "enables the farmers to go off to war."

WAR!! Would the farmers all die? And because the President needed men to fight the war, did that mean our wizened gardener was at war too? I thought about the gardener's wrath. Did that anger have something to do with the war? Was that what war was all about? I began to worry and wondered again what this war was all about.

I knew tonight when I went to bed I would pray for the men to stop fighting and I would pray for the way life used to be, all peaceful and nice.

.   .   .

During the war period a small book for war bonds was issued by the government. Little 10 cent stamps (like the free S&H green stamp system) were purchased to fill in the pages. When the book was filled with $18 worth of stamps, it matured in 10 years and was redeemable for $25.

We thought that was exciting, but it took forever to fill one page. Miss Hayes had a system award. One stamp a week for each girl, but girls were awarded bonus stamps for good behavior, for being punctual and for general housework. Beverly and Amy earned the most. As Amy said, "Miss Hayes gave me a lot because I was well-behaved."

That was true, but we knew Miss Hayes favored Amy! Also at that time in the military service, men and women were given the option of purchasing these bonds, which most of them agreed to. If they didn't they were looked upon as not being patriotic. Six or eight dollars was taken out of their salary each month. Back then, war bonds were the thing to do. It was considered the best investment around. My only war bond matured before me! But seriously, I felt it was one of my biggest accomplishments. Just think, $7 free!

I think I just plowed the money back into my savings account. And when I got married, I had $25 more than Joe. So I used to kid, "He married me for my money!"

Chapter 12

No One Wins In War

Oh say can you see . . .
Oh say yee ni . . . songs of war!
listen carefully

During the war years when I was around 9 years old, we would play this tricky song game. Our national anthem started with words, "Oh say can you see" and if anyone heard the national anthem we were supposed to stop what we were doing and stand at attention till the song was over. That was to show our patriotism.

Coincidentally, a well known Japanese song at that time started with, "Oh say yee ni!" Two or three of us would go up to an unsuspecting girl sitting down and start singing, "Oh say . . ." the surprised girl would look up and quickly stand at attention. With a big smile we'd finish the song with, "yee ni." Bursting into laughter, we'd cry out, "Oh you like the Japanese!" Flustered the girl's face would turn bright red and she'd be furious, which made us laugh even harder. In a unison fashion we'd chant, "We tricked you. We tricked you!" Some girls would come close to tears so we'd quickly give them another chance at this game. Their anxious face would break out in a winning smile for this time they had guessed right. We never knew when we'd be approached. Once behind my back, I heard the familiar strains of, "Oh say." I hesitated. What should I do, I thought. I'll just sit here and see what happens, and of course the inevitable happened. The girls teased, "Oh you like the Japanese!"

I shot back, "I do not!"

"Then why didn't you stand up?"

"Because," and before I could finish they giggled and

taunted me some more. This game went on day after day until one time a Nursery girl went crying into the house to tell a teacher. Loud cries resounded throughout the playground.

The word went out, "Come in, come in! Miss Hayes wants to talk to us." The girls came running from the playground with question mark faces and we were herded into our specific age groups. We could tell by Miss Hayes' angry expression that this was serious, especially in the middle of the day as announcements were only made at meal times. As we looked around the front yard, we noticed all the teachers were even there! Miss Reber was taken off guard and asked to stop her cooking to come join us. She came running out wiping her hands on her apron! Miss Reber's smile always contrasted sharply with Miss Hayes' sour face.

Each teacher checked their group of girls to make sure everyone was present. We had to wait because one Lok Hin girl was missing. Cries of, "Mary Jane! Mary Jane! Where are you? Miss Hayes wants to talk to us." Finally Mary Jane was found. She had been in the Lok Hin bathroom sitting on the toilet reading.

We stood quietly at attention with our eyes on Miss Hayes. She was standing on the second step of the front porch looking down at us. Looking up at her, she loomed above us like a monstrous hunchback giant. Shooting hard looks around, she surveyed all 35 girls. I recognized that glare and knew we were in serious trouble. With swift venom she blasted us for playing the song game and using the word "Jap!" We gasped the word, "Jap!" We didn't say that! As if she could read our minds Miss Hayes bellowed, "I know all of you have not said that word, but some of you have and each one of you know who you are!" We looked around and wondered who had said it and how Miss Hayes knew. Someone had tattle-taled! She told us that we were not acting like good Christian girls. As we shifted uncomfortably in the hot sun we could see

95

by her intense expression that she was attempting to figure out how we were to be punished. But because she could see that there were so many girls involved she decided the best thing to do was to punish everyone! "Everyone? All at once? How was she going to do that?"

"After dinner and prayer group there will not be any play time and you will go straight to bed," she stated. Moans escaped us as we hated to go to bed early and besides, we had planned to play kick-the-can tonight. Suddenly Miss Hayes raised her voice several levels and boomed, "BE QUIET!" We stopped immediately.

Continuing on, Miss Hayes roared, "I want to hear all of you say out loud, "I will not play that game again."

We all repeated, "I will not play that game again."

She added, "I will not say Jap again." And like soldiers obeying the sergeant's orders we again mimicked her. Miss Hayes concluded sternly, "You may go now."

Going our separate ways we whispered amongst ourselves, "Wow, she's really mad."

"Yeah."

"I don't know why, do you?" The game was just for fun, that's all."

"Yeah," we chorused. "It was just for fun."

.   .   .

Going to bed early that night, I sighed. I wasn't sleepy. But then I started daydreaming and my thoughts turned to Earnest, Miss Reber's cute nephew who was in the Navy and stationed at Treasure Island. He was the most fun person we ever played with. What if Miss Hayes had thought to withhold our punishment for the weekend when Earnest came to visit Miss Reber? That would have been devastating because I had a crush on Earnest. All the girls liked him, but I think I liked him the most.

Some weekends Miss Reber would know the time Earnest was arriving. I'd then rally the girls together and yell, "Come on, let's see if we can see Earnest coming."

From our vantage point on the hill, we could see at a distance of about two long city blocks. When we spied a man striding in our directions, we would know it was him, for he was the only one around the countryside who had on a white sailor cap.

Earnest w/ Donna Mae & Margie

Shouts rang out, "Earnest is h—e—r—e. Earnest is h—e—r—e."

The Nursery girls poured down the driveway to greet him. The two youngest sisters, Donna Mae and Margie stretched out their eager arms and cried, "Hold me Earnest, hold me."

With an enormous smile on his freckled face he joyously swept them up. Their faces beamed. With a heart- warming sight and like the Pied Piper he was, we all trailed behind them.

One weekend we had been playing the game keep-away, when we saw Earnest coming up the driveway. A cottage girl, Pansy (Edna and Nora's oldest sister) threw the ball at Earnest and like a professional baseball player he caught it single-handed. Pansy shouted, "Do you want to play keep away?" Before Earnest had a chance to answer all the girls charged in his direction. Back and forth the ball flew from one girl to the next as Earnest darted from each girl grabbing the ball and running off, with everyone in hot pursuit. Dust flew everywhere.

When the game became too fast and furious for me, I joined the Nursery girls on the sidelines, lending my cheers to whomever had the ball. I liked both sides!

I could see Pansy's flushed face. She seemed to be blushing as she pried the ball from Earnest's clenched fist. I wondered if Earnest liked her? How could he not, as Pansy was an attractive girl and very feminine. But now as she pranced around she was just like Edna, a tomboy. Yet she even looked prettier!

And now I could see that Pansy and the girls were slowing down. Earnest sensing his victory raised his arm and smiled proudly.

We all looked at the winner and our eyes froze. There was silence, for Earnest's uniform was completely covered with dust. Worst of all, the cuff on his uniform was ripped and gaped like an angry hole.

Earnest was crestfallen. Miss Reber, who was not fond of sewing took out the Home's sewing machine and hesitantly proceeded to make the treadle hum. It sounded like she knew what she was doing. "Miss Reber," we asked cautiously, "How is the uniform?"

"Well, I'm no seamstress," she replied. "I hope this passes inspection."

We all felt so bad and we were so embarrassed. Later that day, we heard Miss Hayes had lectured Earnest on being so rough with us. Poor Earnest, it was not even his fault.

That evening in bed I knew that there was one compensation for this type of punishment; I could at least daydream in peace. I began to giggle as I recalled his face and I quickly pulled the covers over my head to stifle my sounds, for that day his eyebrows and eyelashes had turned completely grey with dust. He looked like a blinking ghost!

Finally I started to doze off thinking of Earnest and the upcoming weekend. The weekend arrived, but Earnest didn't come. Even though I knew he did not come every weekend, I still questioned Miss Reber.

I stood at the kitchen door and called in, "Miss Reber, where's Earnest?"

A bustling Miss Reber answered hurriedly, "He's not coming."

I felt my heart drop, but I asked, "Why not?"

"I don't remember Nona. I don't think he had a pass." I wondered if he had been denied a pass because of us! Poor Earnest.

I sighed. A weekend without Earnest was like a balloon with no air!

And this weekend the Cottage girls would miss out on the fun of walking him to the Greyhound bus depot in town. For on Sunday evenings when it was time for Earnest to return to the base, they would always use the excuse, "Miss Hayes we're leaving for C.E. now (Christian Endeavor, a church study program). Miss Hayes knowingly went along with their escapade and even got a kick out of it! And the lucky Cottage girls would be off, leaving the rest of us behind yelling at the top of our lungs, "GOOD-BYE EARNEST."

It was during this war period, a Mrs. Peterson came to live briefly with us. Her job was to be Miss Reber's assistant. Like Earnest, Mrs. Peterson was also in the service. We were amazed. A woman who could go off to war! She must be brave! We never met her husband as he was in the military and stationed overseas. But what Mrs. Peterson brought with her to the Home changed my life forever, for I fell in love. Pure love, my heart went out to her three-month old son, Donnie. He was the sweetest, cutest human being I'd ever seen, with silk blond hair and twinkling eyes. When he smiled and cooed, my whole body warmed with tenderness. We helped feed him and played with him every time he was awake. He loved us back.

Once I asked Mrs. Peterson if I could bathe him. She

was skeptical, but she was so busy in the kitchen that she agreed. But only if I could find someone to help me. I was elated. I rounded up Carol and together we listened attentively as Mrs. Peterson gave us careful instructions on how to hold a slippery baby in the bathtub.

Donnie didn't care who was bathing him as long as he could play forever. When we finally pulled the plug, he bent over earnestly and patted the water with his happy hands till there was absolutely nothing left. After we dried him, powdered him and diapered him and gave him his warm bottle of milk, we watched him fall blissfully asleep. I felt like a real mom. Mrs. Peterson was proud of us.

On Donnie's 1-year-old birthday, Mrs. Peterson baked him a cake with white frosting. Everyone gathered around for this festive occasion. And like Donnie, most of us had never seen a birthday cake with a candle, but we knew to call out, "Blow out the candle, Donnie." He was puzzled. His mother leaned forward to help him, but before she could, Donnie's chubby little hand reached out and grabbed a handful of the creamy frosting. He was perplexed but he proudly extended his hand for us to see.

"Eat it," we laughed.

When the day came for Mrs. Peterson and Donnie to leave, gloom settled in while I held back my tears, for now I was much too old to cry, especially in front of anyone. The only thing that made me feel better was that Donnie would finally get to see his father.

.   .   .

And now looking back on these war years, there were many lessons learned. I learned about the different feelings of love, about men fighting, about patriotism, and about enemies. But most of all I learned about killing, for soon a tragedy of war would come into our lives and leave a lasting impression on my mind.

Chapter 13

The Four Letter Word

slang — cuss — dirty words!
picked up here and who knows where!
a mouthful of soap!

Was it Miss Hayes' passion for opera or was it her hope for us to derive some cultural lessons that kept us silent at lunch time?

Whatever the reason, we disliked the heavy, dramatic music that swelled and reverberated and left our ears jumbled and our minds confused? We tried to catch Miss Hayes' enthusiasm when she would tell us of a dramatic overture about to occur. We listened, but we weren't moved. Only Miss Hayes' face lit up.

During these "opera lunches" we couldn't talk. If we needed something passed to us, we whispered. But as usual some girls at adjacent tables away from Miss Hayes' scrutinizing eyes would forget and when that happened Miss Hayes' eyes shot out like an arrow from a bow. She pinpointed the embarrassed culprit immediately. Fortunately for us, lunch time didn't last long.

Today at lunch our dessert was one of our favorites — fruit cocktail. As we scooped up the last drop of the delicious syrup, we wished for more. But unlike the regular food, dessert was not set on the table. Our dessert was brought to us from the kitchen individually in a small dish by the girl assigned to clear our table, so there were no seconds.

The Home received this fruit from a cannery in San Jose. Each season when the cannery opened a sampling of cans to inspect, the Home reaped the contents of the fruit.

As was the procedure, Miss Reber picked a couple of girls from the kitchen crew to assist and accompany her to pick up the fruit. She made sure each worker was given a chance to see the cannery.

To us, it was like an exciting field trip and a good break from our everyday routine.

We were so lucky to have all this fruit, but when Miss Reber returned she had to work overtime lining the shelves of the pantry with sterilized jars of canned apricots, peaches and pears.

And now a happy girl at our table held up her spoon for all of us to see, as she had the one fruit we all wanted — the half of a bright cherry! We giggled enviously as we watched her pop her prize cherry into her mouth.

Suddenly we heard the familiar "ding-ding" from Miss Hayes' spoon. We stiffened. Had we been too loud? But we could see with relief that she had not heard our giggles.

"Today," she announced, "There will be no naps!"

Jubilated, "Yeahs," escaped us before Miss Hayes could finish. We clapped our hands.

"DING DING." This time Miss Hayes' tapping sounded urgent. "But we will all pull weeds instead!"

"Oh!" our faces fell.

For weed pulling was hard work!

Miss Hayes scanned our downcast faces and exclaimed, "If you all do a good job pulling weeds there will be a surprise. The Nursery girls will work with Miss Chew, the Starlights with Miss Davies, and the Lok Hins and Cottage girls will work with me. When you're through Miss Reber will hand out your surprise."

Our faces beamed.

We pulled and pulled while the teachers and the older girls hoed. The sun's intense rays bored into our backs so deeply we felt our bones would melt. Perspiration rolled off our faces and the teachers stopped and wiped their brows. Back and forth we carted the weeds in an old wooden wheelbarrow onto the playground. Each year the ground looked so neat after we had pulled those tall, tough weeds.

Laura & Harlan

I remembered once when I was in the Nursery and how excited I got as the pathway leading to the playground, when pulled, appeared normal, for once again I could see the familiar ground. I patted the bare ground affectionately as if an old friend had reappeared.

And now we continued to clean the playground and

Miss Chew

the surrounding area thoroughly. We were glad the garden area across the driveway had no weeds as the gardener always took care of that area. Hours later the playground was covered with huge mounds of limp weeds. The younger girls had fun running and plopping into the soft mounds. The teachers laughed as they watched and some girls showed off for the teachers by running extra fast, but the teachers soon chided them to stop and to get back to work.

In the late afternoon, we were tired and flushed as we had pulled every single weed from our land. Miss Reber had gone downtown for our surprise and we watched anxiously for the car to return. She honked the horn loudly as she rounded the bend and we scattered and hid behind the mounds.

Miss Reber called out, "Where are you?" No answer. "No one's here?" We giggled softly.

"Well, I guess no one wants their surprise."

With happy shrieks we rushed forward eagerly as her

103

hand dived into the grocery bag and she pulled out the ultimate surprise — popsicles, big bombers and fudgesicles.

"Oh boy!" we yelled. "Thank you Miss Reber." We were elated. Just as we finished our treat, Bingo came stumbling out of the main house. Her tongue was lolling, her eyes were red and her hand was clutching her throat.

Startled, we called out, "What happened? What's the matter?"

Gasping and grabbing her throat, she sputtered, "I swore at Miss Hayes because I didn't want to pull weeds and she washed my mouth out."

We stared at Bernice who was nicknamed Bingo because her last name was Bing.

Bingo came to the Home full of deep seated emotions. She was outspoken and fiery. She disliked Miss Hayes with a passion and once when Bingo had been scolded by Miss Hayes she came storming in to tell us how she hated everything about the Home, especially Miss Hayes and Miss Chew.

One girl piped up, "Everything?"

Bingo stopped and answered, "Yes, everything!" But she thought and answered, "Well, not everything. I like Miss Reber because she listens to me."

She was so mad, her eyes blazed like fireworks and she furiously stated she was going to run away! No one had ever ran away and a girl inquired, "Where would you go?"

"San Francisco," she answered confidently. "I have an uncle there. I'll go live with him. It's much better there. Here you can't do anything."

I remember thinking, "I don't want Bingo to go." I liked her. She was a fair person and not afraid to speak her mind. I had never seen anyone so explosive. It amazed me. I was surprised Bingo thought that way because I liked the Home and had never thought otherwise. And now she looked at us defiantly and pityingly as if we were naive and childish and continued, "Miss Hayes tells you to pull weeds and you obey her and then all she gives you is ice cream!"

We looked at each other and no one uttered a word.

Now watching her writhe in pain we felt numb from her outburst, but we felt compassion and we questioned her in unison, "You had your mouth washed out?"

With her tongue hanging out and her body heaving she barely nodded, yes. Holding her stomach she continued, "Miss Hayes washed my mouth out with soap!"

"With soap?" we asked. "Ugh!" Our faces mirrored her pain. "I feel sick like I'm going to throw up." We watched her bend over as she heaved out a mouthful of sickening foamy saliva.

"And she made me swallow some!" she croaked.

"Oui Yuck!" we made a face and echoed, "You had to swallow the soap?"

"Yeah."

"What did it taste like?" we asked. "Terrible!"

We encouraged Bingo to sit down and questioned, "How did she wash your mouth?"

"She used a toothbrush and scrubbed my mouth real hard."

"What did you say? What was the swear word?" we asked, as we ogled her decrepit form.

"I can't tell you."

Surprised, we asked, "Why not?"

"Because Miss Hayes warned me if I ever say that word again she will punish me worse." Looking around she lowered her voice and whispered, "She's a mean old . . ." She stopped before she completed the sentence.

That evening while washing my face, I looked at my bar of Ivory soap and wondered how it would taste. Gingerly, I picked up the soap and put it in my mouth. "Oui..yuck..spit..spat," I couldn't get the suffocating taste out of my mouth quick enough. As I quickly swished my mouth with water, I wondered what word could be so bad to be punished like that? Then I remembered a word Frances taught me. While playing outside, Frances asked me, "Do you want to know what the word is when a man does it to a woman?"

I looked at Frances and was surprised at the question but quickly answered, "Yeah, what is it?"

"It's a word that rhymes with suck but it starts with an F."

"An F?"

"Yes."

"You mean it's fu...fuuu...fuck?"

"Shhh, not so loud."

"It's fuck?" I asked her in disbelief.

"Yep, that's what it's called," Frances answered knowledgeably.

"That's all?" I asked, "Are you sure?"

"Yeah, I'm sure."

"But it doesn't sound like a regular word."

"It is, Frances answered assuredly, "and that's what it means."

So I thought to myself, "That must really be a bad word and maybe that word got Bingo in trouble." I wondered if she even knew what she was saying!

Laying in bed on the Starlight porch that evening, I thought of the nickname we used for our Starlight teacher Miss Bertha Mae Davies. We called Miss Davies, "B-M!" Maybe Bingo said that word! But then I thought Bingo probably knew a lot of bad words.

Exhausted from the day, I collapsed in bed and was fast asleep. Suddenly I woke up with a start and looked around but couldn't see anything. The room was pitch black though the dark sky spangled with stars. I could hear the steady breathing of the tired girls in deep slumber and my earns tuned into someone's snoring. I wondered why I was so fully awake. Could it have been an owl's persistent hoots? Recalling the days hectic events I had forgotten to say my prayers.

We were taught to say our prayers every night (in bed) before we fell asleep. If I forgot or fell asleep, I wouldn't feel right and besides, God who was up in heaven could always see what I was doing!

I closed my eyes and thanked God for the day and ended my prayer with a plea, "Please don't let the teachers be so mean to Bingo and let Bingo like the Home and please don't let her run away. Thank you God. Amen."

But I couldn't get back to sleep as the word I learned from Frances seemed stuck in my mind, for I was thinking about my mother.

I remembered a frequent visitor mother used to have. He was always impeccably dressed in a white suit with a white panama hat. His tan face contrasted sharply with his outfit.

One day while mother was busy in the kitchen there was a knock at our front door. She told me to answer the door. Before me stood the man in white. Mother called out and told me to let him in. Then mother told me to stay in the kitchen. I did and the two of them went into the bedroom.

The next thing I recall was being seated in a chair in the bedroom next to the bed. Mother and the man were on top of the bed and they were moving back and forth. I noticed our white bedspread merging with his white jacket. They did not notice me. I looked around the dark room and my eyes took in the only other piece of furniture — our dresser. With nothing else to do, I sat quietly in my chair, studying the sparse room.

And now I wondered if what my mother and the man did was the bad word? I tossed in bed, closed my eyes tighter in hopes of falling back to sleep and thought, maybe tomorrow I'll ask Bingo about this.

Chapter 14

Mmm, mmm

chopsticks, criss-cross, laughs
awkward, dropsies - small hands learn
Chinese customs - fun

When the smell of dinner reached me, I stood up from my game of hopscotch and sniffed the air and uttered, "What's that I smell?"

The air was pungent with delicious scents. What was Miss Reber creating in the kitchen? I inhaled deeply and the wonderful aroma made me hungry. Quickly, I bent down and retrieved my hopscotch chain and dropped it in my sunsuit pocket.

"Mmm-mmm," I hummed as I rushed into the playroom and stopped at the kitchen door and hungrily asked, "What's cooking?"

Surprised, Miss Reber's flushed face looked up from the sputtering fry pans and with a good-natured laugh replied, "liver!"

"Ugh-oh," my face fell. Disappointed I repeated, "liver!" I was fooled again! "Why does liver smell so good and taste so bad?" I thought. Miss Reber kept two cat bowls on the kitchen floor, to the left of the stove, and I could see our two cats devouring the tough strips of raw liver. It looked terrible. As their sharp teeth chomped down on the side of their mouth, the sounds of gnashing and the flipping of the bloody liver strips splashed on the floor. Gulping the liver down the cats looked up at Miss Reber appreciatively and proceeded to chomp on the other side of their mouth.

Miss Reber smiled affectionately at the cats and saw my queasy face and in a teasing manner called out to me as I left, "Tomorrow will be Chinese dinner - no liver Nona!" I felt better, for I loved Chinese food even more than I loved Miss Reber's thrifty, economical dinners of which she carefully prepared with the rationed food stamps delegated to each household during the war. Her beloved spaghetti, sautéed brains with scrambled eggs and her famous braised tongue with delicate herbs and the newest dish, tripe simmered in tomato sauce were some of her thrifty creations! One popular dish was her macaroni and cheese with a creamy sauce that felt so wonderfully smooth in our hungry mouths. Miss Reber would cut chunks of golden cheese for the casserole from a humongous round of cheese, which was the size of the station wagon's tire. Every time I saw this round cheese I would think, "If Miss Reber ever needed another tire for the car she could use the cheese!"

The next day Miss Chew, who alternated cooking Chinese meals with Mrs. Lee, had the girls on kitchen duty meticulously slice the home grown zucchini along with the store-bought onions. Miss Chew cut the meat with the Chinese butcher knife which she had sharpened using the bottom of a ceramic rice bowl. Holding the knife in her right hand the rice bowl in her left, she alternately and expertly scraped the edge of the knife against the bottom of the bowl. The rapid flashing blade was a class act, but the scraping sounds pierced our eardrums. In a few seconds the razor sharp butcher knife was ready to slice the beef paper thin. The aroma of the vegetable oil with the garlic heating in the two restaurant size woks wafted to the outdoors, filling the grounds with the tantalizing fragrance we all loved.

"Mmm," our faces beamed. "Chinese dinner tonight," we exclaimed. Tonight instead of a regular prayer, the teacher said we would sing Break Thou The Bread of Life. We sighed, as it always took longer to sing a song. But we bowed our heads and sang. Some of us I'm sure was thinking about the food!

"Break thou the bread of Life, / Dear Lord to me, / As thou didst break the loaves beside the sea / Beyond the sacred page / I see thee Lord / My spirit pants for thee / Oh living word. Amen."

When we sang the grace the words or phrases didn't mean much to us. But the one word that stood out in our minds, was the word "pants." That word would make us snicker, and as we sat down, we looked at each other in a playful mirth. But we stopped before the teacher caught on. One time a teacher asked us, "Why are you laughing?" We looked at her and with a straight face and with complete innocence replied, "Nothing!" They eventually realized what it was, and after that we changed to singing, "Praise God from whom all blessings flow..." And that song was even longer!

After singing we sat down eagerly for Chinese food which was prepared only twice a week. The girl whose duty it was to clear the table after each meal assisted with the teacher's chair as she sat down. The teacher always sat at the head of the table. The girl also served the teacher hot tea, which she poured from the kitchen. The steaming cup of tea with its saucer was placed to the right of the teacher's plate.

All our dishes were of an institutional style. They were durable and white with two dark green lines circling the edge of the plates and cups. We were served a cup of milk with each meal. But once I had lost about two pounds so I had to drink two cups of milk for the entire month. I didn't like that! And why I lost weight I don't know, but I was always skinny. There was always a silver metal pitcher of ice water in front of the oldest girl whose duty it was to fill our cups when needed. The teacher dished out the aromatic zucchini with sliced beef, which Miss Chew had flavored with a pinch of sugar which always amazed me because I didn't think that sugar would blend with the vegetables and meat. The oldest girl scooped a bowl of steaming white rice and passed it to the teacher. She in turn spooned on the simmered, home grown tomatoes seasoned with fresh ginger and mashed cubes of fermented bean cake. We were taught the proper Chinese way of eating, holding the bowl to our mouth with one hand and with our other hand we held the chopsticks and shoveled the rice into our eager mouths. "Mmm," the taste was delicious. The down-to-earth flavor made this one of our favorite dishes.

Shoveling the rice into our mouth was quick and easy and considered good manners. It was considered impolite to eat rice any other way. The difficult part was picking up the vegetables with our chopsticks. The Nursery girls used the shorter red plastic chopsticks, while the rest of the girls used the longer brown wooden chopsticks and the teachers used the smooth ivory, the hardest ones to handle, which Mrs. Lee had once brought back from China. We ate with chopsticks during all of our Chinese meals but as always there would be some who took longer to master the skill. Laughs came as chopsticks crisscrossed and food fell off our sticks back into our bowls.

I was sitting to the right of Miss Chew and successfully eating my dinner when Miss Chew asked, "Nona, why are you using your left hand?"

Huh? I looked at Miss Chew and my roving eyes quickly fanned our round table. The girls were all using their right hands.

I shrugged, "I don't know, it just feels better."

"Nona, you have to learn to use your right hand. It's too dangerous to eat left handed with chopsticks, you might poke someone's eyes."

I switched hands and my chopsticks crisscrossed. I couldn't pick up the zucchini. Finally my chopsticks fell on the floor and rolled under the table.

Frustrated, I said, "Excuse me Miss Chew."

We had to ask permission each time we left the table. Miss Chew nodded her approval. I got off my stool to retrieve my chopsticks. As I came up from under the table I bumped my head, "Ouch!" I cried and rubbed my head. The girls looked at Miss Chew's stern face, but she was smiling, so it was a sign that it was all right to laugh. The girls at my table laughed uproariously. I looked at their laughing faces and though my head still hurt, I broke into laughter also. Wiping my chopsticks on the corner of my blue cotton napkin, I shuddered because we had to use our napkins for a week. I was afraid my napkin would be the dirtiest by then!

When we were given our clean colored napkins we all rolled our napkin neatly into our own art deco animal napkin ring holder. We knew exactly which napkin ring holder each girl was assigned. After each meal we placed our napkin rings in special shelves. Each girl had their own little square. The dining room girls then closed the narrow cupboard. Everything was very orderly. My napkin holder was a blue Scottish dog. My dog was nice and quiet unlike the Home's new German Shepherd who was an oversized puppy from the Guide Dogs for the Blind. Miss Hayes who had wanted a dog, invited the instructor to visit the Home and after her visit our Home was chosen by the school to raise the puppy so the dog could adjust to a crowd of people. This was an honor for the Home.

I was afraid of his playful actions even though he was on a long metal leash attached to a pulley line which reached from the end of the front house over to the unused water tower. To avoid him I would take the long way around to the lower half of the circled flower bed to get to the main house. I was always fearful that the chain might snap and he'd bound after me. The other girls loved the dog, especially Jenny. She would play with him while I watched from a safe distance. But once I petted him and his enthusiasm nearly knocked me over which made me more fearful than ever! One day the instructor brought a trained dog for us to observe. She explained that she and four other women from the Tilted Acres mansion in Los Gatos wanted to help with the war effort and their contribution was to train dogs for returning service men who had been blinded by the tragic effects of war. So in 1942 they formed the first school of trained dogs in the Bay Area.

She told us these dogs would be the eyes for our veterans. Fascinated we watched as she secured a special harness on the dog. Ready to demonstrate she closed her eyes as the dog led her up the stairs. The dog stopped at each step until the woman found her footing. The dog repeated the process going down the stairs. The dog patiently waited, constantly observing and sensing her reactions. Next, the woman placed a large box in the middle of the yard and closed her eyes again. As she directed the dog towards the box, we held our breath. When the dog was in front of the box it stopped. It was the smartest dog I'd ever seen. I loved that dog and when the instructor asked if we would like to help raise their dogs everyone's arms shot up, even mine! We waited anxiously for the day we would have our own seeing eye dog. When the appointed day arrived our dog bounded out of the car like a racehorse and wanted to play. It was so rambunctious, I backed away, disappointed. And now I looked at my napkin ring dog and thought how silly I was to compare it with a real dog but our guide dog was a wearisome thing!

Proceeding to eat again my right hand felt clumsy. I had no control over the chopsticks. Finally, with Miss Chew's approval, I transferred my zucchini into my rice bowl and shoveled the food into my mouth and finished every bite and not one delectable morsel was left. Occasionally a lone piece of rice was left on a girls' face and someone would quip, "Are you saving that rice for your auntie?"

"Mmm," I put my bowl down and placed the

chopsticks across the top of the plate carefully so they wouldn't roll and that also indicated I desired more food. If I had positioned my chopsticks across the middle, that would be a sign I had enough.

With hopeful eyes I glanced at Miss Chew. I could not ask for a second helping as that was not proper. She saw my plate and my hopeful expression and asked, "Nona, would you like seconds?"

"Yes please," I replied eagerly. I placed my chopsticks to my right and passed my plate. All of us had seconds; there were never any leftovers with Chinese food. As we received our second helping, we always remembered our table manners with a "Thank you, Miss Chew." Our table manners were constantly observed with each meal with quips of, "Sit up straight, don't slouch, don't talk with your mouth full and elbows off the table." Occasionally a Caucasian guest from The Board of Missions or the church would visit and sometimes stay for dinner, especially if it was Chinese, and they always commented on our excellent manners. After the main course, the assigned girl cleared the table for our dessert. Ending each Chinese dinner was a large plate of refreshing orange wedges. I always wished we could have Miss Chew's macaroon cookies. They were my favorite dessert. About twice a year she treated us, using her own money to bake the most delicious cookies I'd ever eaten. The fresh smelling dough and tantalizing coconut perfumed the large white kitchen. Peeking in once, about four girls and I huddled secretly watching at the kitchen door. Miss Chew was rolling the dough out to the last spoonful. Obscured by the dark playroom behind us, we ooh'd and aahed silently, each girl vying for a better view. Suddenly, Miss Reber, who was in the kitchen watching Miss Chew's activities called out, "All right girls, she's done. Go outside to play!" Goggle-eyed, we jumped back and took off. That evening for dessert we savored each morsel and took small bites to prolong the pleasure. Enjoyable sounds filled the room as Miss

Chew's rare smile lit up her face.

After dinner, I felt satisfied, when I remembered that soon it would be our once a month meal of jook, plain rice simmered in water to form a tasteless gruel. Doing this, we saved the money from that meal and sent it to the starving children in another country. When Miss Hayes said the prayer for the hungry children, I wondered how there could be starving children in the world. And anytime we complained about our food, we were reminded of the starving children, but we really couldn't understand. Would hungry children like the grey eggplant which looked like garden slugs, or dried thistle artichokes, or even the thick tapioca pudding filled with pin-point size balls that never squished in half when chewed. Maybe we could send the food we didn't like to the starving children.

Sometimes we suspected that we had jook because the Home was low in funds. At that time we were constantly reminded to turn off the lights whenever we left a room as the electric bill was astronomically high.

Climbing into bed after a meal of jook, my stomach felt empty and I had hunger pangs. Lying in bed I thought, "What if I hadn't eaten any dinner or lunch or even breakfast with the terrible mush, then I would be really starved. I began to understand and closed my eyes. I thought of the pensive-face snapshot in Miss Hayes office displayed on the narrow ledge above her desk. It portrayed a young, sad-looking Korean girl. One night after a dinner of jook, Miss Hayes asked if we wanted to adopt her.

"Adopt her?" we questioned.

"Yes, she grinned, "we would be her family."

Our interest mounted. "But how can we adopt her? What would we do? She lives so far away." Questions came pouring forth while the thought of this special little girl arriving caused a ripple of excitement.

We waited for Miss Hayes' answer and she replied,

"We would write her letters and send her pictures and each month I would take some money from your allowance and send it to the orphanage."

Oh, we looked at one another and realized the girl would not be coming to the Home; Miss Hayes had tricked us!

Miss Hayes continued, "Now I'd like to see a show of hands if you agree." She looked expectantly around the silent room, that was a few minutes ago full of charged enthusiasm. We hesitated, but since no one wanted to be un-Christian like, all hands were raised and we adopted the girl. It now seemed obvious because of our good deed Miss Hayes could now include this story in her annual report to the National Board of Missions.

Months later Miss Hayes received a "thank you" note from the girl and when she read the letter to us her face glowed. We caught her happiness, but I could see she derived more pleasure from this sharing than we did.

Thinking about her while lying in bed that evening, I wondered why Miss Hayes used her method to gain our support. I know we would have all helped the little girl and I thought Miss Hayes likes her more than us.

Closing my eyes in prayer, I prayed, "Dear God, thank you for the day and for my food. Please help the hungry children, especially our adopted girl and please give her someone to play with. Thank you God, Amen."

Thinking back to the incident of adoption, I remembered when some visitors to the Home mentioned something about adoption. I recalled our stricken responses, "Oh no, we wouldn't ever want to be adopted, because that would mean we'd be separated and we would have to leave all our friends."

After that there was no more mention of adoption.

117

Chapter 15

The Winds That Made Me Late

safe in bed, I cringe
skeleton branches whipping
mounds of fallen leaves

The night winds howled. Looking up at the black angry sky from the Starlight porch I could see the tall trees swaying from side to side and I was glad I was snuggled securely in my warm bed. Heavy grey clouds swept across the sky and covered all the millions of stars that usually twinkled.

I thought of my 6th grade teacher Mrs. Campbell who frequently and proudly reminded us that Los Gatos had the best weather in the world second only to Aswan, Egypt. But tonight I wondered if Egypt had weather like this!

Front of Lok Hin, Cottage building
on right. ca 1937

I could barely hear the Cottage girls running to their cottage for bed. The gale force winds blew their shrill voices into the whistling night.

118

"Older Girls"
2nd row: Emma, right
3rd row: left, Pansy, Emily, Ethel
4th row: Rhoda, right
5th row: Bernice Lee, left

Tonight they could not leisurely stroll across the front yard giggling and singing the popular song, When the Moon Comes over the Mountain. No, tonight the moon was hidden. There was no moonlight to brighten the pathway leading to their cottage but, perhaps, the wayward moon was shining elsewhere across the ocean and as far away as China where Mrs. Lee grew up.

During the annual "Moon Festival" celebration on the 15th day of the 8th lunar month, when the moon was fully round and luminous, Mrs. Lee and her girls strolled through the grounds under the moon's silvery shadows as Mrs. Lee retold the ancient folk story of "The Lady in the Moon." It was a sad love story as the lady could not marry the man she loved, for she had been betrothed to another man as planned by her family; which was the ritual of match-making in China. Heartbroken, the lovers planned to meet in another lifetime once a year when the moon was at its fullest.

The enraptured girls listened and, gazing at the moon, some actually believed they could see the lady while the story was being told! The privileged Lok Hins also feasted on slivers of moon cakes filled with a salted egg yolk and sweet tasting beans. Each was given a glazed cookie in the shape of a fish which was tied with a red string, so they could play with it the next day. But they could never resist and ate the cookie that evening. But one time I asked a Lok Hin girl to save me a piece of her cookie. "No," she replied. "Please," I pleaded earnestly, "I've never had one." She shook her head.

"Please, just a little bite?" Finally she relented. I was overjoyed.

The next morning when I saw my "bite," it was so minute. I didn't think I could even taste it but I did. This Chinese cookie was delicious with just a hint of sweetness.

As Mrs. Lee and the older girls continued on we could hear the dim sounds of their questions while we laid in bed looking at the full moon. But soon our eyes grew heavy and we drifted off dreaming of the time we'd be the lucky Lok Hin girls.

And now it looked like the heavy clouds would burst. If that happened, the rain coupled with the howling winds would blow through the screened windows and dampen their cottage beds! For safety measures the girls would cover their beds with their raincoats! When the girls complained about their damp beds the teachers would tell them good naturedly, "Fresh air is good for you!" That explanation never pacified the girls but they accepted the fact that the Home didn't have any funds for windows. Besides the raincoats did keep them dry.

The wind was blowing furiously and rattling the windows. I shivered and slid further down into my covers. I closed my eyes and thanked God I was safe inside my bed.

The next morning I opened my sleepy eyes and looked up at the sky. It was overcast but the winds had subsided slightly. At breakfast this morning was one of my favorite foods — a soft boiled egg which would slide down my throat with ease. It was so different from mush. I wish we could have eggs everyday. The older girl poured the scalding hot chocolate into our mugs. We loved this beverage but a wrinkled skin would form on top of the hot chocolate in the pitcher and we'd cringe and hope it wouldn't go into our mug.

My job this month after breakfast each morning was to sweep the front porch. The large porch wrapped around the front entrance and ran along both sides of the main house. Sweeping the porch was a job I enjoyed. I swept the front section porch and as I came around to the left side of the porch I couldn't believe what had happened. The giant oak tree had shed its leaves over the entire side porch. I heaved a big sigh. I swept and swept and got one area clean when the wind would pick up and all the unswept leaves would dance and scatter across the clean area. I panicked, "How am I going to sweep all these leaves fighting this wind?" I was going to be late for school again. Frantically, I tried to sweep faster and almost had the leaves cleared when the wind started up again. Finally, I finished sweeping and raced off to find Miss Davies to inspect my job.

Miss Davies checked the side and front porch and as she walked to the left side the wind had subsided. Following behind her we turned the corner and approached the side and my face dropped, for the leaves were back and had already formed little mounds in the corner.

Miss Davies looked at me incredulously and in a hollow voice asked, "Did you sweep this side of the porch?"

My mouth quivered from exhaustion as I nodded, "Yes." She looked at me skeptically and I stammered, "I did but the..."

"Nona, I'm surprised, you can do better than that," she said, disbelieving me.

I re-swept and re-swept trying to out race the wind. My hands were red and sore and small calluses were starting to form. Meanwhile girls were leaving for school and I felt panicked. I raced back and forth so hard, I failed to notice Miss Reber.

"What's the matter Nona?"

"I have to sweep the porch, but the leaves keep flying back."

"Put the broom away and get ready for school."

"But Miss Davies said..."

"I'll explain to her. Just go Nona."

I could barely mumble a grateful "thank you" I was so tired. I ran up the stairs to change into my school dress. It was quiet. "Has everyone left?" I thought nervously. I dashed down to the kitchen to grab my lunch and saw my bag — it was the only one left on the table. I was scared. I didn't want to walk to school by myself.

Miss Saylor, a new elementary school teacher, had recently moved into a brown shingled house on Johnson Avenue. She would leave her Doberman pinscher running free in the front yard while she was at school for the day. It seemed the dog would lie in wait for us because the minute it saw us it would jump over the low wire fence and chase us. My friends and I would scream in terror until the older girls came to protect us. As we ran ahead, they ran behind yelling, "Go home! Go home!" The dog would stop and make a forward move but the brave girls continued on in their loud voices, "Go home!" and the dog retreated.

Coming up to the house my heart was pounding wildly. I was in front of the Baggerly's secluded gardens surrounded by a high hedge, I peered into an opening hoping Mrs. Baggerly would be in her front yard to assist me. But she was nowhere in sight.

Directly across the street the dog was lying down on the front porch and his one ear perked up as he heard me. Then he saw me and both ears shot up and with a leap he sailed over the fence and came loping towards me. Petrified, I couldn't yell, "Go home!" Screaming and with tears spilling down my face, I ran down the steep dirt grade full of little pebbles. I couldn't look back because I might fall or slip. At the bottom I looked back and the dog wasn't behind me. Surprised, I looked up and the dog was standing at the top looking down at me with his head cocked to one side. I wasn't even sure if he was wondering why I was screaming or if he was mocking me. I didn't care. I was just relieved. Catching my breath, but still unnerved I ran on. Walking towards me was a Mexican mother with her baby and child. She stopped and asked if I was lost. I hesitated and almost said no, but embarrassed by my tears I said, "Yes."

"Where are you going?" "To school."

She gave me instructions and her finger pointed towards the direction of the shortcut, a route Miss Hayes forbade us to use. "Do you understand the directions?" she asked sympathetically.

"Yes," I replied wiping my face.

Thanking her I started walking towards the short cut. "Should I go that way?" I thought. I turned around and the helpful lady was watching me, so I couldn't go the regular way. Besides I felt it was okay to go that way because she was a grown up; a grown up wouldn't give me bad advice. The wind had stopped and the sun was shining brightly. I felt better as I ran down the pathway. I spied the shiny poison oak on the bank and remembered when I had poison oak so bad I was quarantined in the infirmary and had to stay home from school twice. Each time I had to go to Dr. Harder for heat treatment, to dry the oozing pus. Huge scabs formed and fell off my face, leaving it raw and bleeding. As I ran past the pretty plants, I was afraid to look at them.

To my right, in the distance, I passed the high school football field and could see the players exercising. No one was in view as I approached the enclosed iron bridge. There was a wide gap. As I stepped onto the bridge's wooden plank I could see the rushing water under my feet. As it cascaded and bubbled over the glistening rocks, I thought that must be the dangerous spot Miss Hayes talked about. Little brown finches twittered cheerfully and flew in amongst the barren trees. The beautiful scenery dried my tears. I wished I could stay, it was so tranquil.

I strode up the steep bank from the bridge and came in from the back of the school. No one was around except the school's mascot — a mellow, mustard-colored dog called Chief. Slowly he greeted me with his big tail wagging.

"Hi Chief," I said as I patted his head. I could feel the strength of the dog emanating from his neck and I felt proud I wasn't afraid of this dog.

This was the second time I was late for school. I was not too scared but was apprehensive. The hallways were quiet as I raced up the stairs to the second floor of the Spanish style elementary school. My footsteps echoed in the cool halls. I entered my classroom and could see the class was already in session. The teacher, Mrs. Campbell, was standing and talking with a student. She looked at me surprised and asked why I was late.

"Because I had a job to do and..."

Before I could finish the sentence she motioned for me to sit down.

Relieved, I collapsed at my desk and realized how tired and thirsty I was. I wished I could be excused to go to the water fountain. I passed the fountain on the way in but didn't stop, afraid I'd be even later.

Excitement was felt entering the classroom as the entire school was planning a special assembly and each class was to participate. For over a month our class had worked on a song about our school dog, Chief. As eager students raised their hands, Mrs. Campbell would use their suggestions to add a rhyme or word to the song. Every day we rehearsed and when we were ready for the melody, the musical 5th grade teacher, Miss Cangamela, was called in to help.

One day, Karl, the smartest student in class, raised his hand and asked if Chief could participate. Mrs. Campbell's intent face brightened, and she asked, "What could he do?"

Karl emphatically suggested, "He could bark." We all laughed. "Or he could just stand on stage."

After much discussion, Mrs. Campbell agreed, but added, "Let's not tell anyone of our plan as we all know sometimes Chief wanders off the grounds and he could be at the creek lapping the cool water or even strolling around town greeting all the townspeople."

I looked over at Karl's enthusiastic face. Karl always amazed me. I always wondered how he knew all the answers. Every time the teacher posed a question, his hand was raised even before the question was completely out of the teacher's mouth.

Jumping ahead in time, in 1966, 50 years later, my questions were answered. Karl told me his parents were older than most parents and they had provided the right type of home atmosphere for learning.

He also added that some students referred to him as a

nerd, so he had to learn how to control himself. Karl a nerd? Never — just one smart guy. Besides, the word "nerd" sounds terrible. In those days, I don't think they used that term.

Years later Karl received a full four-year scholarship to Stanford!

And now back to our school mascot, Chief, whom we all loved. He belonged to a student in school. Chief always followed him to school and stayed outside all day. He was a good watch dog. If a stranger walked on the school grounds, he instinctively barked and never stopped until the school teacher on yard-duty checked it out and told him it was okay. At lunch time some students would feed him sandwiches and we shrieked when he gobbled them down hungrily. I wished I could throw him my dry jam sandwich, but if anyone saw me, they might tell a teacher at the Home and I'd be in big trouble. Once Paula was seen throwing her sandwich in the garbage can and Carol told Miss Chew. Paula was severely scolded. Months later when the movie Cinderella was in town we all attended except Paula! Paula was younger than Carol and me and one time when she was a preschooler she had been naughty so she was caged just like Ida.

When we came home from school, Paula was still in the cage sound asleep. I don't know how long she was caged, but the teacher had forgotten her!

The big day for our special assembly came and we could not find Chief anywhere. Disappointed our class assembled on stage by sopranos, altos, and bass, at three different levels. The audience was silent. We were ready to begin when Miss Cangamela lifted her arms to proceed, but there was a commotion in the wings. She stopped and out came Chief being led by the collar by Mrs. Campbell. Surprised laughter resounded through the auditorium, as Chief was never allowed inside the school building. He laid down obediently in the front row. And now we were ready. Miss Cangamela lifted her arms and motioned to the piano player and we proudly sang:

The mascot of our school / who seldom breaks a rule / is a big yellow dog, Chief by name / A good dog — he's been found / When he's on the school grounds and with the children he would often join the games / chorus: oh dog Chief ever faithful / when he's gone we'll all be filled with grief / he's our pal / he is kind / we'll never ever find / a better friend then old dog Chief.

Like a well behaved dog, he stayed through the entire song. He looked at the audience and his ears perked up each time he heard us sing his name. We looked at Chief adoringly and we could barely keep from laughing when his ears twitched. Everyone in the audience applauded again and again and we glowed with appreciation.

That was the best assembly we'd ever had. After the assembly everyone gathered outside the auditorium near the bell tower hugging and patting Chief. He loved the attention, his tail never stopped wagging. His thick tail thumped from side to side causing dust to fly and making us laugh.

I noticed Miss Saylor looking at us. She was such a nice, quiet teacher. No one had the heart to tell her that her dog was mean.

Miss Saylor looked at me and said, "You seem to like dogs."

I looked up from patting Chief, and solemnly answered, "I like Chief."

Dog, Chief; Beverly, 2ⁿᵈ row, 2ⁿᵈ from left Nona, 2ⁿᵈ row, 2ⁿᵈ from right; Karl, 3ʳᵈ row, 3ʳᵈ from right

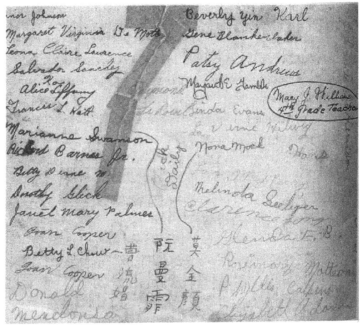

Los Gatos - 1943

Chapter 16

Is It 4 O'clock Yet?

behold, each flower
a vision of God's beauty
renewing one's faith

As the war continued we had a surplus of vegetable seeds. During our summer school vacation, Miss Hayes decided to give each older girl, if she desired, a small section for her own garden. The area designated was raised and wedged by a stone wall, located behind the oldest girls' cottage quarters. We were granted the privilege of maintaining our own garden with no supervision from a teacher. We had our choice of any vegetables we wanted and when they matured we could eat them fresh from the garden or give them to Miss Reber for cooking! We were jubilant, our very own garden. But Miss Hayes warned us that this was a big responsibility and we had to water our own plants every day no matter what we were doing. We could not neglect our garden or we would be in big trouble. She asked for a show of hands of those who wanted their own garden and hands shot up quickly as we all anticipated this adventure.

Standing in line for our seeds, Miss Hayes told us there were radishes, lettuce, carrots, zucchini and many more vegetable seeds to choose from. And then by surprise she added, "I also have 4 o'clock flower seeds."

My ears perked up like a donkey. "4 o'clock flowers?" I questioned, "What's that?"

"Little pink flowers that open up at 4 o'clock in the afternoon!" Miss Hayes answered. I was enthralled and amazed. I couldn't believe that flowers knew how to tell time! I was in a dilemma. "What should I do?" I wanted to be patriotic and plant a vegetable like everyone else, but I was intrigued by a flower that could tell time.

Miss Hayes jarred my thoughts. "Which seeds do you want Nona?"

"Uh," I looked at the black round 4 o'clock seeds and held one between my finger and squeezed it. I was amazed it was so hard, I couldn't even dent it!

"Hurry and make up your mind Nona," Miss Hayes voice hit me again.

"I don't know. I want both!" I lamented. She looked at me with a half smile.

"You must make up your mind," she said wryly.

Frustrated I answered, "I'll take the 4 o'clock seeds." With my hands squeezed tightly around my seeds, I walked carefully to the garden area.

Miss Hayes then placed us according to how much space we would need for each type of seed. My area was up in front! With sticks we found from the playground we staked off each section and tied off each separate garden with a white string. While the girls were busily planting their vegetable seeds, they'd yell out proudly, "I have my own victory garden!" I looked at them and wished I could join them in their happiness. Carol noticed I wasn't yelling and asked, "What kind of seed are you planting?"

I answered, "They're 4 o'clock seeds." "What's that?"

"They're flowers."

"FLOWERS!" they yelled. "How come?"

I shrugged and replied, "Because these flowers know how to tell time!"

The girls looked at me and giggled. "Tell time? How?"

I shrugged off their questions and didn't let them bother me because I was going to have a flower that was unlike any other flower around!

Soon my flower's leaves branched out strong and sturdy. Small buds formed and were ready to burst. I told Carol, "Any day now my flowers will open and they will know when it's 4 o'clock!" Carol said nothing. She just looked at me in a quizzical way.

As the days went by the buds didn't bloom. I'd water faithfully and then go off to play. Suddenly right in the middle of playing jacks on a hot afternoon, it dawned on me. I wondered what time it was. I rushed up from the playground and stopped at the kitchen door and breathlessly asked, "Miss Reber, what time is it?"

Miss Reber answered, "It's about ten minutes to four. Why do you want to know? she asked.

"Because I have to see if my flowers are opened yet!" I answered. I raced up from the kitchen, passed the main house, passed the empty water tank house and the Lok Hin building, and ran down the side of the cottage to the garden. I stared at the buds. Nothing! This happened again and again, then one day I got impatient and went early. I looked at my flowers and they had bloomed! I was shocked. They were pink as Miss Hayes said they would be and they were very small with pointed petals. I was disappointed because they weren't very pretty, and as I bent over to smell them there was no tangible fragrance! All this work for 4 o'clock flowers! Then the truth became apparent, it wasn't even 4 o'clock yet and the flowers were open. I was disillusioned. I wondered why Miss Hayes had told me such a story.

Frustrated, I went to the kitchen to tell Miss Reber. "Miss Reber, why did my flowers open before 4 o'clock?" Miss Reber, trying to keep from laughing, chuckled, "4 o'clock flowers are named 4 o'clock because they open around 4 o'clock in the afternoon."

"Don't they open AT 4 o'clock?"

Amused, Miss Reber answered, "Sometimes, if we're lucky!" Dejected, I looked at Miss Reber and told her I didn't like the flowers now and I wished I had planted a vegetable because at least I wouldn't have wasted my time and I could at least eat the vegetables!

Miss Reber looked at my down cast face and said, "Go

look at your garden again Nona."

"Why?"

"Go ahead Nona," she said gently, but firmly, "Go take another look at your garden."

I left with my head hung down. I slowly walked outside and scuffed up the fine dirt and watched it vanish in the air. Feeling low, I approached the garden and did as Miss Reber told me. I looked at my garden again.

I saw bright pink flowers right in front and noticed how attractive they looked framed amongst the different shades of greenery. They were the only plant that was colorful in the victory garden! Each sturdy stem with its dark green leaves had a cluster of bright perky little flowers in the center. As I looked closer I realized each little flower was shaped like a star. I was amazed, they were so perfect, like a gift from God! As my eyes lingered on my flowers I began to feel differently and realized why Miss Reber sent me out to look at my flowers.

I could see how beautiful and special a flower could be if I took the time to really look at it. I felt so much better and I was glad I had picked the 4 o'clock flowers because they did what nature intended — they beautified the garden, and they made me happy!

And if they made me happy then everyone who passed by would be happy and maybe, just maybe, forget the horrors of the war, even if only for a moment.

Chapter 17

One Pink Rose

...and the child asked
"Is my mother still living?"
but no one answered...

When I was around 8 years of age and in the Starlight group our usual Sunday naptime became a game of daring adventure! Because we disliked taking naps, we rarely slept. Instead we would lie and wait for the familiar sound of a visitor's car spitting gravel as it wound and crunched its way up the driveway and slowly circled the enormous flower bed before coming to a stop in front of the main house.

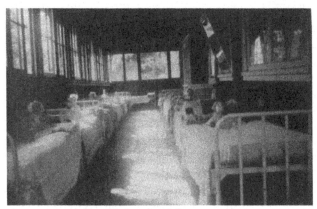

Starlight sleeping porch

When the car's engine stopped, that's when the adventure would begin! The girls whose beds were directly beneath the high screened windows overlooking the front garden and driveway, and whom wanted to join in the game, would quickly stand up in bed to see which visitor had arrived. One had to be cautious because if you were caught doing this you would most likely be punished by staying in bed an hour longer. We never knew when a teacher would sneak up and check on us.

The cars would sometimes be filled with someone's relatives or a single parent. We always wondered who would be the lucky girl. After a while we knew which car belonged to which parent. Elizabeth's (name changed to protect privacy of any living relatives) father was an exception. Whenever he visited he walked from the downtown bus station. I felt sorry for him as many days would be sweltering and he was always dressed so warmly. Though his outfit was somber looking, he looked like he had just come from a festive celebration in old China. His top was a black long sleeve shirt and he wore a traditional skirt which graced his ankles. He was the only father who dressed in such a fashion. He was also the only parent who didn't visit in the living room; instead he chose to visit in the private comforts of the garden. We thought he was strange and also secretive because he and Elizabeth would converse in hushed tones and whenever we got near their area they'd stop talking and retreat further into the garden.

When some curious girls asked a teacher why he was so different, the only reply was not to bother them. So we were glad Elizabeth never told on us, although we never thought she would, but she was a very moody individual.

I never knew why Elizabeth's father was different. But years later when I was a young adult I heard Elizabeth had committed suicide. I was shocked. Poor Elizabeth. I wondered why. Could we or the teachers have helped her back then?

Now my friend, Amy who was a cute, little carefree individual was one of the most fortunate ones for her father visited frequently. It seemed every Sunday the girls peeking out the window would whisper excitedly, "Amy your father's here." And Amy's eyes would twinkle and she would smile as her little dimple amplified her happiness. The girls would quickly plop back in bed to feign sleep.

Shortly after, we could hear the teacher on duty coming up the stairs. Quietly she opened the connecting French door leading from the Starlights dressing room to the porch and tiptoed to Amy's bed and softly nudged a supposedly sleeping Amy! Amy's entire face dimpled with excitement as she hastily dressed.

Watching Amy's happy face, I was reminded of the time when some of us Starlights had been discussing the reason why they came to live at the Home. Amy had told us that her mother had died when she was born.

There was silence, when a girl implored, "She died because of you?"

"Yes," Amy smiled.

An uneasiness surrounded us. I wondered why Amy was smiling. I thought she would be sad. But in Amy's smile I saw sadness. It was as if she wanted reassurance that it was not her fault and that everything was okay.

Though we didn't try to comprehend the reason for her mother's death or Amy's part in it, we felt empathy and we gave our reassuring expressions and sympathetic hearts.

When Amy's father came to visit he would occasionally give her money, almost a whole dollar! That was a lot of money and because Amy and I were "good friends" I asked her if I could have some money.

As she hesitated I pleaded, "Please just a dime or a nickel."

Once I got a dime! I looked at my small silver dime and studied the woman's beautiful profile, turned it around and looked at the thinness of the coin. I toyed with it some more and finally put it away, placing it carefully in the corner of my dresser. It was my treasure and very precious to me.

And now as I watched Amy leave, I thought how fortunate she was to be able to visit with her father in the living room, where they would not only enjoy the view, but also see my favorite mountain, El Sereno. I loved that mountain which had a forest of evergreens high atop the mountain. Lucky them. In the living room the side windows had built in flowered cushions where the older girls sat at prayer time. Outside this expansive window stood the century old oak tree which once made me late for school. Its massive branches rose up majestically and darkened the ground below, while the sturdy limbs extended across the entire side yard. How beautiful it all looked!

Separate woven bamboo chairs from China were for the teachers and an antique blue velvet loveseat was for the older girls. Two small woven rocking chairs were for which ever Starlight girls reached the living room first! The youngest girls sat on a large Oriental rug which covered the hardwood floor. Miss Hayes had her own special padded lounge style chair. Adjacent to her chair was a shiny mahogany dining table. Centered on this table was a magnificent bouquet of fresh cut flowers from our garden, picked and arranged each Saturday afternoon with loving care by Miss Hayes. These assorted flowers, which I loved, were always displayed for our Saturday evening prayer time and for any Sunday visitors. This table was waxed with care by a Cottage girl whose job it was for the month to clean the living room. Everyone wanted this job because it was a privilege to be in this magnificent room which we were not permitted to enter during the week.

As time passed, I accepted the fact that my mother was not coming to visit and I rarely thought of her, although I would have been elated if I had been roused from my nap with the wonderful phrase, "Nona get up; your mother's here!"

Once when I was in the Nursery group I was awakened with, "Nona, you've got visitors!"

I rushed down to the living room wondering, hoping, thinking maybe, just maybe...On entering the living room my face dropped for a strange woman wearing a black hat and a matching overcoat was sitting and waiting for me. Alongside her were two other strangers. Looking at my perplexed face, the teacher told me, "Nona this is your grandmother and your aunt and uncle." My grandmother's tan weathered face and piercing black eyes looked coldly at me. I glanced at her anxiously. She glared at me and demanded in broken English, "Say hello, you no talk?"

Her grammar surprised me, but composing myself, I responded timidly, "Hello grandma," and noticed my voice trembled.

"Speak louder!" said my uncle. "Hello grandma!" I blurted. "Louder! She can't hear you."

I hollered, **"HELLO GRANDMA!"** and felt my face heat up.

My expressionless grandmother grunted a barely audible, "Hello."

She seemed to be searching for clues as she scrutinized my apprehensive face. Feeling uncomfortable and self conscious with her penetrating eyes aimed at my face, I realized my relatives were indifferent and uncaring strangers. I felt let down. I thought a relative would smile and be happy to see me. I was frightened of them and wondered if this was what it was like to have a family. I observed them and could see no physical similarities between us except our black hair. My uncle did have big eyes. I felt uncomfortable and almost wished the visit would end.

During our visit my relatives sat motionless and from the corner of my eye I could see them looking around the room. They seemed ill at ease. I wondered what they were thinking.

Even though I didn't enjoy my time with them, I experienced another type of comfort, for I was proud, because like the other girls, I too had visitors! Plus I didn't have to take a nap and I could enjoy the living room and sit on the prized rocking chair and once again admire the flowers.

Each succeeding visit which were infrequent, about once or twice a year (if that) were awkward, especially when I entered the room. For if I forgot to greet grandma promptly and properly I was harshly reprimanded by her. I learned to quickly perform like a nervous actress at her first audition. My body would stiffen and my voice would quiver loudly, "HELLO GRANDMA!"

After a while doing this annoyed grandma for now she could not even scold me! On one visit I did find the courage to ask them if my mother was still living. They looked at me suspiciously and turned to each other and conversed rapidly in Chinese amongst themselves. Observing them, I felt left out and excluded from their world.

When they turned to me, my uncle answered in English, "Go ask a teacher!" I was bewildered and wondered why no one would tell me. I felt like no one cared.

When my relatives got up to leave, I stood up quickly and remembered the manners taught by the teachers. Even though I didn't feel like saying anything, I politely said my goodbyes.

As I watched them leave, I felt an emptiness inside me and sighed, it seemed I would never know about my mother.

As it came closer to the month of May, I knew a special Sunday would be coming up. Mother's Day, and at the Home it was a day to look forward to, for although we were without our mothers, we always honored them.

And when Mother's Day finally dawned, I dressed quickly and dashed outside to the garden. Today I knew I would find Miss Hayes at the rose garden.

As I approached the garden I could see a glow of color. Blooms of brilliant red, warm pink and startling yellow contrasted alongside the clean white roses. Each rose rich and full reached out for the sun's nurturing caress. Dew glistened on each hearty bush. This section of our varied gardens was Miss Hayes' pride and joy. She nourished and lavished love on each bush like a doting parent. I sensed Miss Hayes would have been happier if she had been a full time gardener! Miss Hayes' tall angular form was bent over carefully snipping the fragrant red and white roses. The sharp clicks of her snippers were heard clearly in the morning's silence. Each prized rose was laid carefully in her flat rattan basket. Standing on the perimeter of the garden was akin to being on holy ground. The gentle breeze captured the essence of her treasured roses. Its delicate bouquet lingered in the air just long enough for me to enjoy. I filled my lungs with the luxury of the sweet smelling air. The fragrance sharpened my senses, and I felt blessed. No one was permitted inside the rose garden, except Miss Hayes and the gardener although we could stand outside the carefully laid out rocks bordering the rose garden and admire the velvet roses. On Mother's Day it was Miss Hayes' ritual to pin a special rose on each girl's Sunday dress. Girls whose mothers were living wore red roses and girls whose mothers were deceased wore white roses.

As usual this was always a dilemma for me. On previous Mother's Days I had always worn a red rose and felt a sense of closeness to my invisible mother.

139

Outside the rose   "Inside" the
garden ca 1937   zinnia garden

So this Sunday morning, before I asked Miss Hayes my usual question, I greeted her.

"Good morning, Miss Hayes."

Miss Hayes stopped cutting and without straightening up, smiled in my direction, "Good morning, Nona."

And then I once again posed the question, although I knew what her answer would probably be. "Miss Hayes, is my mother alive?"

"I told you before Nona, I don't know. Did you ask your relatives?"

I nodded "yes" and replied, "They don't know either."

Anxiously, I asked Miss Hayes, "Can I please wear a red rose?"

Miss Hayes paused and scanned my hopeful face. She turned and glanced at the basket of red and white roses. Canvassing her large assortment of rose bushes, she strode over to a bush at the corner of the garden and expertly snipped a pink rose! Beaming, she handed it to me and said, "Wear this one Nona!"

I was ecstatic. "Thank you Miss Hayes."

I walked to church with my pretty pink rose pinned to my Sunday dress and felt content.

All the girls looked so festive with their own rose pinned snugly in place. Lost in my thoughts, I felt lucky indeed as I thought my pink rose looked almost red, when Carol walked up to me and questioned, "Why are you wearing a pink rose?'

I craned my neck to smell my rose and matter-of-factly quipped, "Because I don't know if my mother is dead or alive." She looked at me wordlessly. I admired Carol's red rose and bent over to inhale the fragrance.

"Like it?" she bubbled.

"Oh yeah, it smells so good. I love roses. They're my favorite flowers."

Carol was lucky even though her mother never visited her, she at least knew her mother was alive.

Chapter 18

The White House

in depth of spirit
lies God's church, breathing deeply
I enter within

The old witch's house was across the street, kiddie corner from our Presbyterian church. We called her a witch because she was mean and scary looking, and when she yelled at us, we could see her toothless mouth. Her unkempt straggly hair hung over her Halloween face.

Overgrown shrubs partially concealed her small wooden house which was covered with cracked and peeling white paint. Adjacent to her house was a huge parking lot for both the Presbyterian and Methodist churches. It seemed appropriate that her house was the only one on the block as who would want to live next door to a witch!

We walked gingerly each Sunday past her spooky house hoping to avoid her.

But one Sunday we could see small flames darting like fire- flies along the edge of her barren lot. Peering through the dead shrubbery we could see her holding a rolled up newspaper with flames spilling forth from the other end. Forgetting our fears we asked, "What are you doing?" Ignoring us, she continued torching the ground.

Some girl whispered, "See, she's a real witch!" Suddenly she whirled and hissed, "Get out of here." Frightened we could see her raging eyes and what appeared to be a yellow tooth.

But one bold girl questioned her again and she snapped, "I'm killing ants."

"Ants!" we whispered, "she's crazy!"

Someone called out urgently, "Let's go." And we scampered off to Sunday school.

Running across the street out white church came into view, its color brilliant and pure. Our nondescript church resembled a stucco house. It was set close to the street with one lone graceful peppertree in front, its delicate yellow flowers attracting the honey bees and making it a challenge to enter the church. It paled in comparison with the First Church of Christ Science which had stately columns and a lush green lawn. Our church was next door to the Methodist church which had a steeple that soared to the sky with a grand entrance of rose bushes and a towering redwood tree. The outward appearances of the other churches were impressive, but I liked our church, the interior floor plan was shaped like a cross. The arrangement was ideal with the choir at the top rising majestically behind the minister. Behind the choir were large brass pipes projecting from the organ. The pipes nearly reached the ceiling and when the choir stood up to sing they looked like a host of heavenly descended angels! As we entered the church, organ music reverberated throughout and I was enveloped in a state of holy reverence. I felt peaceful.

Long-time members and regular church-goers like us were seated at our usual pews. By habit, the ushers knew which pew each worshipper preferred. I enjoyed watching the dignified ushers seat the congregation. The ladies were clothed in their hats and gloves, freshly pressed linens and elegant dresses. The men's perfectly tailored suits looked impeccable. The last person seated was the minister's gracious wife. Every Sunday she greeted us upon entering the church with a sincere smile and a warm handshake.

The Church service was long and laborious but it was interesting to watch the minister's manners. He read the Scriptures in a modulated voice and carefully laid the satin ribbon bookmark across the page and closed the Bible in his precise ways. Then he walked back to sit down in his deeply carved chair with his black robe swaying regally behind him. He never wavered from this routine. I never understood his sermons; although I tried.

But the part that captured my interest was the ritual and analogy of communion Sunday. The little cut up square pieces of fresh white bread reminded me of soft baby pillows! When the ushers passed the platter of heaping bread around the fresh aroma was heavenly. How I wished I could take one like the grown-ups. The round serving trays which held petite glasses of purple juice in separate cubicles was a challenge for the ushers to hold the tray steady. One elderly usher was always shaky and the glasses clanged together like wind chimes. I felt embarrassed and sorry for him.

When the minister, Mr. Hammock, held up a single piece of bread and said, "Take, eat, this is my body which has been broken for you," all the congregation solemnly opened their mouths and partook. He finished the ceremony by holding up a single glass and concluded with, "Drink this in remembrance of me." I watched fascinated as all the members tilted their glasses and in the hush of the church you could hear their swallows. In unison they placed their glasses in the special receptacle attached to each pew and the sound echoed throughout the church. After the ceremony there was an incredible amount of leftover bread and juice. I wondered what happened to them.

One Sunday my curiosity got the best of me and when everyone stood up and had their eyes closed in prayer I reached out and dipped my finger in the residue of the teacher's glass. It was sweet and good. Years later I found out it was grape juice!

The juice reminded me of a section in the Home's garden which we called, "The Garden of Eden." Located in the amaryilla bella dona area were two loquat trees laden with clusters of golden fruit. The strawberry-sized fruit beckoned and tempted us. And the fact that the people in China loved loquats made it more intriguing. But Miss Hayes strict orders were for no one to eat the loquats. We couldn't understand why this was forbidden.

One lazy warm day a group of Starlights wandered into the quiet garden and strolling towards the trees, Amy mused, "I don't know why we can't eat these loquats; I'm sure they're good for us." Carefully fingering a cluster; she broke one loquat off and apprehensively bit into it. Her eyes danced and with a coy smile stated, "It's good, try one." We did and we couldn't stop. The fruit was wonderfully sweet, but filled with a large slippery pit which made some of us gag. Like cubs attracted to honey we gorged on another and another and before we realized what we had done, the branch was bare! Frightened we ran off.

Miss Hayes must have been alerted by the gardener. Because, like Adam in the Bible, Amy got in trouble and had to sit in the corner and ponder her sinful ways and why the fruit was forbidden to us. For dinner that evening the guilty Starlights ate only dry bread and water. Secretly we didn't feel too bad as the fruit was well worth it! In fact we were fortunate as dinner that evening was the least popular dish of all; navy beans! Ugh, navy beans. How could Earnest eat them?

As my mind shifted back to church, I realized my eyes were focusing on the shimmering stained glass windows, made more beautiful and enchanting by the sun's dancing rays.

Occasionally Mr. Hammock's dry wit would come through and my eyes would dart from the stain glass to the faces of the laughing listeners and that would lighten my boredom.

But Paula who was now the youngest Nursery girl would usually nod off. When that happened we would nudge her before Miss Hayes saw her or else Paula would have to take a longer nap. In Miss Hayes estimation, Paula was just too tired to stay awake in church!

Seated in front of us each Sunday was a middle-aged couple with granite faces. Sometimes this frosty face woman would wear a fur piece of orange-tone foxes wrapped around her shoulders.

We would whisper, "Are they real?"

"Yeah," they're real."

"But they look like babies," I exclaimed with sadness.

The poor little foxes, how could this woman adorn herself with dead animals?

One Sunday a girl "fong pei" (passed gas) and while the odor permeated our section we sucked in our breath, made faces and looked around for the culprit as suppressed giggles escaped us. The teacher's stern look quieted us. The granite-face couple sat composed during the episode without the faintest detection of emotion.

Miss Davies who loved to sing was in the church choir and she sat in the front row with a good view of us and fortunately for us, she seemed not to notice the commotion.

Seated behind Miss Davies in the choir was Mr. Yacco whom we all liked. He lived on another hill beyond us on a one-lane dirt road which wound through the mountain. After church he and his family would drive past a group of us trudging home and honk the horn and call out, "Would you like a ride?" Delighted we'd squeeze in, four or six at one time and we'd be so crammed we could hardly breathe.

Mr. Yacco would tell us about the trains he was making and he could see we were interested. In a few weeks they would be completed and he would have us up to his home.

The day came and Miss Hayes announced the good news. She reminded us that this was a special outing and to remember our manners and be on our best behavior. When we saw his trains we were speechless, for they were real, complete with an engine and a caboose. Climbing aboard the open boxes, he cautioned us to keep our arms inside the cars and to duck under any low-lying branches. Donning his engineer's cap he drove us around and around his hilltop pulling on the train's bell and tooting the whistle. We were thrilled as the rush of the wind against our bodies and faces felt like freedom. I now looked up at Mr. Yacco sitting in the choir, but he didn't see me. He was listening attentively to the minister's sermon.

After the sermon it was time for the ushers to pass the collection plate and the younger girls were ready with their shiny pennies. They had a penny for Sunday school and a penny for church. Once when I was in the Nursery group Miss Bankes handed out the pennies and remarked, "Shiny pennies make nice gifts for the Lord." When she turned around she saw us busily shining our pennies on the rug! That was the only time I remembered that her eyes twinkled!

Each Sunday we had felt a glow as our pennies gleamed amongst all the other sealed pledges and occasional currency.

As we got older, around 13 years of age, we returned to church in the evening for Christian Endeavor (CE) study groups. Because CE was in the evening, Miss Reber drove us to class and back. We alternated going to CE because there was so many of us and not enough room in the car for all of us.

A fair skinned blonde hair boy named George, whom I had known for years, was in my group. He was so unusually pale, he looked transparent! His eyebrows and eyelashes were almost invisible against his face. One day at Sunday School he sat next to me on a large couch which sat four to five people. There were only three of us on the couch, but he sat so close it made me feel uncomfortable. I asked, "Can't you move over?"

"Oh," he murmured nonchalantly.

That day in class the teacher asked who was coming to CE. Hands raised and George looked at me and he

147

asked with controlled excitement, "Are you coming?"

I answered, "Yes," so he eagerly raised his hand. I then realized he liked me. I was surprised but I didn't feel anything for him. In fact, some of his actions bothered me. I felt he was overly eager to please in whatever the situation was. After that incident I'd look the other way and try to ignore George or sit down after he was seated. One Sunday I had on a crepe dress in a beautiful shade of red with a white design which made my face radiate. George sat across the room directly opposite me and stared at me throughout the entire class. Self conscious, I looked down at my lap, looked up again and he'd still be looking at me. I groaned inwardly and wished he'd stop staring. I wondered why he wasn't attracted to the other Caucasian girls, who wore fancy dresses and lace trimmed socks with shiny patent leather shoes.

A teacher from the Home came into class to see which girls were attending CE and George immediately shot up, "Nona's coming." His outspokenness surprised and embarrassed me. The Home teacher was surprised and also realized for the first time that a boy liked me. I saw in her eyes what looked like aggravation because it seemed it might be a burdensome problem!

George trailed behind us as we walked home and I heard him yell, "Nona, I want you to meet my mom."

Mortified, I stopped and said, "Hello."

Catching up with the girls, they started chanting, "Oh, George likes you! George likes you!"

"I know," I protested, "but I don't like him."

That night after CE George asked me if he could walk me home. I thought it was funny because we lived so far away and said, "You want to walk me home?"

"Sure, why not?"

"Because we live over a mile away." "That's okay."

I told him we had a ride home. I was so relieved to see Miss Reber waiting for us.

But there was one young man in the congregation

many girls were enamored by — Hugh Peniston, who was pleasant with an engaging smile. He was extremely handsome, and would have been perfect for Hollywood on the big screen as a movie idol.

The man I had a crush on I kept a secret. He was a bass singer, Don Logie, in the church choir. He was the youngest, but by far the biggest, broadest man in the group. When he sang solos I was entranced. I'd never heard anyone sing with such depth and power. He was so good he had his own once a week radio program.

Occasionally we were permitted to stay inside the house and listen to a special radio program. But when Don Logie's program was on, we were allowed to listen every week. I would gaze mesmerized at the gracefully arched radio which sat on its own small table in the corner of the reception room and listen to him sing his theme song, "I'd climb the highest mountain / If I knew that when I climbed that mountain / I'd find you / I'd swim the deepest ocean / If I knew that when I swam that ocean / I'd find you." I listened intently and each word found its way into my heart! And when the song ended I was left with a rapturous feeling. I was mesmerized. But no one knew how I felt. In fact, the other girls lost interest in listening. I'd say, "Come on, don't you want to hear Don Logie sing?"

"Nah."

I was the only one listening! On his program you could call in to request a song and I was so bewitched I sneaked into the office and looked up his number in the phone book, dialed, and when he answered I was speechless! I thought his kind mom, whom I knew, would answer; but he answered, "Hello!" and the sound of his voice seemed to swell from the bowels of the earth.

I gasped, "Is this Don Logie?"

"Yes," he answered.

Faint with anticipation, I stammered, "Umm, umm."

"Yes," his voice boomed.

I stammered again and my face flushed. My tongue was tied, but I finally managed to ask, "I want to request a song." I felt his surprise as he waited silently, but then, I heard footsteps in the quiet house. Frightened, I hung up the phone and ran off.

The following Sunday when I saw him in church I was so self conscious, I could hardly look at him. I was afraid if he saw my face it would give me away! But of course, he didn't even know I existed.

I now looked at the church-goers coming in and saw his mom. She was tall and stately, an attractive woman, with a generous heart.

I thought of the day she had invited the girls to her home for a boxed luncheon. In her backyard we picnicked on her lush lawn and I felt the luxury of her quiet elegant surroundings. We said our silent prayers and opened our bakery boxes. Inside each box was a chicken salad sandwich with the freshest bread we'd ever seen or felt and were surprised to see there was no crust on the bread! It was magic in our mouths as we had never tasted anything quite like this. Mrs. Logie asked if anyone wanted another sandwich. We glanced at each other too timid to say yes.

She asked again and we all nodded silently. She was taken back by our ravenous appetites but was pleased as she and her friend bustled busily in the kitchen.

Walking by the kitchen door my heart quickened as I glimpsed Don sitting at the kitchen table and realized how different he looked without his choir robe. He had on a white tee shirt and his head was bent down. He seemed ill at ease because of all the girls in the house and did not look at us. He spoke briefly to his mom, put his plaid shirt on and left by the back door. I was disappointed he left, but now I was not distracted.

After lunch, Mrs. Logie took us to the five and ten cent store. She gave each of us 20 cents and we could buy anything we wanted. Our faces glowed with happiness and we thanked her. Our squeals of delight were heard throughout the large store as we ran up and down the aisles and our footsteps thundered on the wooden floors. It was the first time we had been inside the store and the counters of neatly arranged toys and gift items overwhelmed us.

Giggling with excitement we called out, "What are you going to buy?"

"I don't know. How about you?"

Soon girls were paying for their purchases. I was lagging behind.

Mrs. Logie said to me, "We have to leave now."

I looked at her in desperation. Surprised she asked, "Don't you want anything, Nona?"

I nodded, "Yes."

"What is it?"

I hesitated but she encouraged me to show her the item. I walked down an aisle which contained miniature blown glass animals and pointed to a small section filled with pale blue swans which had graceful necks with black dots for eyes.

"Is that what you want?"

"Yes."

"Why don't you buy it?" "Because it costs 25 cents."

Without hesitation, Mrs. Logie picked up a swan, walked to the front counter, placed the extra nickel down, and moved away before I could protest.

My eyes were downcast as the sales girl bagged my fragile swan. I wished it had cost only 20 cents, then Mrs. Logie wouldn't have to spend more money.

On the way home from our shopping spree, I sat back in the car and listened to the chatter of the happy girls as they shared their purchases. Carol asked me, "What did you buy?"

I showed her the swan. "But it cost 25 cents."

"I know, but Mrs. Logie paid for it."

Puzzled, she questioned, "Why didn't you get something for 20 cents?"

151

"Because I didn't like anything and if I bought something I'd just be wasting my money."

Silently I wondered why I did what I did. Was I selfish, greedy or worst of all impolite? I sighed, why did I feel like this? I should be more happy, but coupled with a sense of guilt was this nagging feeling of being upset with myself.

While sorting through the pile of glass swans, I had set aside the best one, with well defined eyes and a perfectly smooth body with no rough edges. But when Mrs. Logie picked a swan for me, she just took the closest one to her. I wished I could have been brave and pointed to the one I had admired.

Sunday School class

Once again I opened my bag and peeked inside. The petite swan was beautiful even though it had one bulging eye that drooped. But did that really matter? I thought of Mrs. Logie's kindness and smiled.

I now looked across the way from where Mrs. Logie was seated in her favorite pew and then back up to Mr. Yacco in the choir loft and I knew what they had done for all of us was one of the many verses Mr. Hammock had read to us in church, "Be ye kind one to another . . . for such is the kingdom of God."

And I knew I would never forget their kindness, nor Mr. Hammock or my church.

Chapter 19

Gold & Silver

...a garden in bloom
or dreams of gold and silver
my wish, "one flower"

Prior to our Chinese study class each week day at the Home, we had to fortify ourselves with a regular afternoon snack. This was not the desirable "all-American" milk and cookie snack, but something we hated with a passion!

This snack smelled bad, tasted bad and practically made us sick. But this was a product of the latest medical finding guaranteed to keep "growing children well." So the Home bought an abundance of this golden liquid.

As we waited in line in the ironing room (adjacent to the laundry room) a heavy offensive odor hung in the air and overpowered the usual scent of harsh laundry soap and Clorox bleach.

Groaning inwardly, we watched with repulsion as each girl in line took their snack and grimaced. When it was my turn, I was face to face with Miss Davies' intense face and she said, "Open your mouth wide, WIDER, steady, don't move. Holding my breath, I opened my mouth as wide as possible while she carefully placed a teaspoonful of slimy cod-liver oil down my throat. I closed my mouth and gagged. I quickly picked up one of the white enamel cups from the counter to help down the heavy slick fish oil, when Miss Davies called out, "Wait Nona, there's some left on the spoon." I cleaned the spoon and nearly vomited. Pure torture. Every drop of this precious oil was not to be wasted because we were told it was extremely expensive.

On a hot day this ritual was worse, because when we grabbed our milk to comfort us, it had turned warm! When that happened, we would race outside to the front yard and run straight to the drinking fountain hoping to dissolve the taste. That helped a little, but the oil and water didn't really mix well and we smelled terrible!

By the time we were through rinsing our mouth, we heard the bell ringing; it was time for Chinese school. We all filed into the (fortunately!) large, airy classroom fortified with cod-liver oil energy.

This all white room adjacent to the living room had windows across the entire back wall. The windows were more expansive than the living room's picture window, but we couldn't enjoy the scenery as our heads were always bent down studying. Mrs. Lee was our sein-saun (teacher), and always greeted us with a smile. Being around her pleasant, quiet disposition was always a pleasure. She almost made us forget how we disliked coming to class for an hour each day after attending our regular public school.

Every day we sat at our assigned tables. The Nursery girls had the smallest round tables, then the Starlights with the next larger tables, while the largest and highest ones were used by the Lok Hin and Cottage girls. And just like a regular classroom, Mrs. Lee had her own desk.

When we were all seated, she began with her usual greeting, "Hello girls."

And we responded, "Hello, Ley-se-nei," (Mrs. Lee).

She then proceeded to outline the lesson plan for the day. Somedays the whole class worked together, but generally we studied in our own separate groups.

Today we were to work together. The chalkboard was covered with Chinese numbers. Mrs. Lee used her long wooden stick and with the grace of a fairy's wand she gently tapped at the characters and our lesson began.

In our precise voices we chanted after her, "Yut, yee, saum, say, mm." (1,2,3,4,5.)

"Everyone say it again," Mrs. Lee's clear voice rang out. And like a record, we started again. We followed her tapping stick as we continued down the column till we reached the number 10.

Mrs. Lee turned to us and in her honey sweet voice said, "That's very good girls." We felt

Mrs. Lee at black board

"That's very good girls." We felt flattered, it was fun to please Mrs. Lee.

Mrs. Lee was born and raised in China and taught us saum- yup (Cantonese), the third dialect of China.

I remembered conversing with my mother in another dialect, so saum-yup was completely new to me.

Mrs. Lee was a slim, petite woman and always wore a traditional cheong-saum, (Chinese dress). She was the only regular teacher who had ever married, so in the classroom, we called her Ley-se-nei. We could tell Mrs. Lee was proud of her marital status. She told us her marriage was arranged by her parents in China. She once showed us a black and white framed picture of her husband which was displayed in her bedroom. He was a big man with a somber face and he wore a black, round cap with a traditional long robe. He had died when their only child, a daughter, was six months old. We were never told how he passed on and although curious, we knew it wouldn't be right to ask. Besides, we wouldn't want to make Mrs. Lee sad.

Today as we finished the number drill, Mrs. Lee announced, "Girls, I am going to give you a Chinese reading book."

Fascinated, we waited as Mrs. Lee and Emma, whom she favored, passed out the lightweight books to each separate table.

A demure Mrs. Lee continued, "Now girls, please don't open your books until everyone gets a copy."

Looking curiously at my book, I noticed it was bound together by a single thread, so I took extra care in handling it as I took a quick peek at the back cover! When everyone received a book, Mrs. Lee instructed us to study the cover.

She continued, "You will see that Chinese books are different from American books; the book opens from the left."

We opened our books and turned the soft cover from the left to the right. It felt strange, but it was easier to handle.

Mrs. Lee surveyed the class, "Now everybody please look at the first word. It starts at the top of the first column to your right and then goes down the page."

Engrossed, we turned the pages slowly and saw columns of foreign-looking words. The handmade pages were thin; almost transparent, like tissue paper. The Chinese words and pictures were printed in black ink. The calligraphy looked confusing. At our regular school, our Dick and Jane reader was so different. The pictures were in color and each page only had two or three sentences. Dick and Jane was much easier to read, with the bold printing and the repetitively used words.

Mrs. Lee watched our expressions and said simply, "Now girls, I will teach you how to read."

I turned the page and was amused to see a picture of a

happy mother and father with little children. Everyone was dressed in comfortable clothing. Another drawing showed two working oxen and some graceful birds flying over a large weeping willow tree. I was intrigued. I could hardly wait to read about this family in China.

Pointing to a Chinese word, Mrs. Lee said, "Bah, Bah" and we repeated, "Bah, Bah," which meant father. Next word was "Ma Mah" meaning mother and we repeated, "Ma Mah." We continued through the entire family. This took a while because in China they had large families and all the married sons and their families lived in the same household. Chinese rhythmic sounds resounded clearly as we earnestly and emphatically mimicked Mrs. Lee.

It was difficult to keep up with her as we began to read. It was impossible to sound a word out. We had to memorize each word and recall how it was written.

One girl raised her hand. "Yes," quipped Mrs. Lee. "Do you have a question?"

"Can we write in the English words next to the Chinese words?"

Astonished, Mrs. Lee murmured, "Oh! Why do you want to do that?"

"Because it's hard to remember how the word sounds," she scowled. "If we can put the sound or meaning down, it will be easier to remember."

Mrs. Lee looked at the girl and her eyes surveyed the classroom. She was thinking and it seemed as if she was going to say yes, but with determination she answered, "No girls, we must learn to read Chinese by looking at the word!"

Deep inside I knew this was going to be hard, very hard for all of us!

Dejected, we looked at each other in silence. Mrs. Lee proceeded with the sentence, but no one could recall the next word.

"Please girls! Try harder!" Finally someone remembered and then another girl called out the next word. We were making progress, but no one could recall the third word and we were at another standstill.

By now my head was beginning to droop. Mrs. Lee bent down and gently asked, "Nona, don't you feel well?"

I looked at Mrs. Lee's worried face and woefully lamented, "I'm all right Mrs. Lee, but this is so hard to read. I'm never going to find out about the family in China!"

Finally in desperation, when Mrs. Lee wasn't looking, some girls very lightly penciled in some English words. When she realized what we had done, she discreetly overlooked it as she realized it was less frustrating for us and we did learn faster. As soon as we memorized the word we erased it. Mrs. Lee was a pacifist; she never wanted any controversy. We felt uneasy disobeying her wishes, but we knew if we hadn't written in the words, we would never have advanced any further, let alone finish our first reader!

A few days later Mrs. Lee had the whole chalkboard covered with calligraphy. "Today," she said, "We are going to learn the Bible verse, John 3:16, in Chinese."

> *For God so loved the world.*
> *that he gave his only begotten Son*
> *that whosoever believeth in Him*
> *should not perish,*
> *but have everlasting life.*

We repeated,

> *"yung why shurn die oy sai guy*
> *sum gee kai curr duek sung gee juer*
> *juer curr goy day, len don faun soon curr gah*
> *mean gee meek mong*
> *yoaw duck wing saung"*

It took over a week to learn and memorize this verse but it became easier and we caught on faster when everyone recited the verse out loud.

After that she taught us different Christmas hymns. It took weeks and weeks of drilling and finally, voices raised on high, we angelically sang Silent Night in Cantonese. Mrs. Lee's eyes sparkled and she twittered happily, "Oh, that's so good girls. That was so pretty."

Interspersed with these religious lessons we were taught our Chinese name. Our name was given to Mrs. Lee by our relatives when we were admitted to the Home.

The entire class participated. We would have these name learning lessons about twice a week.

Mrs. Lee would call out our Chinese names and then translate the English meaning which we would then repeat after her. After we learned our names, she continued to drill us. The faster we responded, the broader Mrs. Lee smiled.

When Rhoda, an older girl, stood up and received her name, Beautiful Moon, she smiled approvingly and enunciated her name with Mrs. Lee. Other girls had expressive names. Bessie's name was Golden Lotus and the sisters, Beverly and Paula, were named Morning Dew and Evening Mist. My sister's name was Golden Lily (Gum Lon). As each name was called, sounds of approval came from all of us. As we listened, we realized Chinese names had beautiful meanings and we enjoyed listening to each girls' given name.

When my name was called I stood up eagerly. Mrs. Lee said, "Nona, your name is Gold and Silver."

161

I was shocked and disappointed. The classroom was quiet. My name was not pretty. It had a funny meaning and besides, it sounded terrible in Chinese. I wished my name had been a beautiful flower. I didn't like my American name and now my Chinese name was worse!

And now I knew instinctively I would have difficulty pronouncing my Chinese name and my American name had a strange sound which made me self-conscious.

Once when I was around six years old, a new teacher at the Home, Miss Bergman, had asked me what my name was and I had answered, "Nunna."

"What?" she replied, "Say it again."

I repeated, "Nunna," and she asked, "How do you spell your name?"

"N-O-N-A," I spelled out.

Surprised she asked, "Don't you know how to pronounce your name?" I looked at her quizzically and she continued, "Your name is NO-na."

I was amazed and pleased that my name actually was easy to say and now it didn't sound so strange. Sheepishly I looked at Miss Bergman and said, "Oh," and ran off. I was so happy. I felt like a new person.

Now looking at Mrs. Lee, I could barely hear her say, "Nona, please say your name, Mock Gum Naaghn." I listened intently and realized when Mrs. Lee called my name, "Nona," it sounded like "Nunna."

Before Mrs. Lee continued with me she paused and explained that in China the family name was always written first and spoken first.

My family name, Mock, was easy and my name Gum, simple, but the last word silver, Naaghn was impossible!

I took a deep breath and copied Mrs. Lee, "Mock Gum Naun."

The girls giggled softly.

"It's Naaghn," repeated Mrs. Lee. "It's hard to say, Mrs. Lee."

"Yes, I know Nona," Mrs. Lee said sympathetically, "please try it again."

I tried to prolong and lower my voice, but after many attempts Naaghn came out sounding like Naun.

Mrs. Lee finally relieved me, "That's all right Nona, you may sit down."

Flustered, I sat down and whispered to Jenny who was next to me, "I don't like my name."

She nodded and I felt consoled.

Trying to pronounce my name reminded me of the story Mrs. Lee told a group of Ming Quong girls (as adults) gathered at Jean Chew's house (a former Ming Quong girl). Mrs. Lee's eyes had twinkled that day and in her sweet way and slight accent she said, "Ah Nona, you were so quiet, you never talked (I was a preschooler then), but one day you did. That morning it had been raining for a long time. You were looking out the window when all of a sudden you spoke in Chinese. You said, "Hard rain fall.""

Mrs. Lee smiled and said, "I wanted to laugh, but I didn't want to discourage you, it was so cute."

.　　.　　.

The next day as we filed into Chinese class, Mrs. Lee took out domino-size pieces of Chinese hard ink and soft bamboo brushes. This was new to us, we were going to learn how to write our name. "Oh, boy!" we clamored, "This looks like fun." Fascinated we watched Mrs. Lee dip a (mo-butt) bamboo brush made from pig's hair into a small container of water and dribble a few drops of water on the hard black ink. With her brush she brushed the ink gently and added another drop of water. Soon the ink was the right consistency and ready to use. We mimicked Mrs. Lee's grip on the brush and carefully stroked the letters of our names. Because I was left handed, the girl next to me had to move over a little. When writing calligraphy each stroke, dot, curve and hook had to be brushed in a certain order and each stroke had to be the correct length. I copied my name Mrs. Lee had written but my strokes did not fit right. The one word I had the most difficulty with was silver; it had 18 strokes. I tried again and again and with each try I sank lower and lower into my chair. As Mrs. Lee stopped at each table, I could hear her giving encouraging words to a girl having trouble writing and sometimes she would praise a girl on how well she was doing. Mrs. Lee looked at my calligraphy and once more showed me how it was done. My tired eyes followed her brush and I marveled at how beautifully she wrote and with such graceful ease. I tried again and the strokes were still out of proportion. My neck was tense and I felt drained. I closed my eyes and my thoughts wandered to Emily who was the only girl not in the classroom because she was taking a nap. Miss Hayes said she was weak and had to rest. I almost wished I could trade places with Emily. I knew if she were here she would learn fast, because she was one of the smartest girls at the Home. She won scholastic awards in high school. Emily, (the middle sister to Ethel and Gloria) often thought Miss Hayes was unfair to her because she was outspoken. Emily would confront Miss Hayes with her complaints.

And according to Emily, when extra household jobs were offered to the Cottage girls, like washing the Nursery and Starlight windows, to earn extra money, Emily was overlooked.

Mental abuse was also used as Miss Hayes compared Pansy's attractiveness against Emily, stating that it would be easy for Pansy to have plenty of boyfriends. This bitter remark annoyed Emily and to this day she can recall it vividly.

The Cottage girls were also not permitted to wear makeup, lipstick or bright colored clothing. All these worldly exteriors was not in keeping with the teacher's ideals of a proper religious upbringing.

But I remembered when Mrs. Lee's face suddenly began to blossom with color. A faint hint of pink appeared on her lips and when some girls told her, "Mrs. Lee your lips look different," she blushed and gushed, "Oh, just a little bit of lipstick, because my face is too pale!" Shortly after Mrs. Lee's eyes even began to dance and took on a new sparkle! For it was rumored that Mrs. Lee liked Mary Jane's (widowed) father! And that was all I knew back then. But many, many years later Mrs. Lee did marry Mary Jane's father and she became Mrs. Linn.

So even though the teachers did not allow the older girls to wear lipstick, nothing was ever said (to my knowledge) about Mrs. Lee's indiscreet conduct! Besides one had to have extremely good eyes to see the new Mrs. Lee!

If Mrs. Lee's lipstick annoyed Miss Hayes, no one knew. But probably the one situation which raised Miss Hayes wrath was when Emily confronted her with a decision she had made about some complimentary show tickets which were sent to the Home. These prized tickets were for the young rising, popular singer, Frank Sinatra, who was to appear at the San Jose Civic Auditorium. The tickets were to be distributed to the Cottage girls who were thrilled, for never in their life did they ever expect to see Frank Sinatra in person. This incredible crooner who left girls swooning and screaming at his performances was the talk of the town and all the students in school, especially the girls, were looking forward to this Hollywood heart throb! And for the Cottage girls to be able to attend with their contemporaries at school was by far the most exciting thing to happen to them!

But Miss Hayes did not see this event as fitting for dignified girls and told the Cottage girls that the cost of the tickets would do more good if they were returned and the monies from the tickets be sent overseas for needy starving families!

None of the terribly disappointed girls would dare disagree with Miss Hayes, except Emily! After the girls dispersed, she confronted Miss Hayes with the fact that the girls should have been given a chance to voice their opinion or to participate in a democratic vote.

About that time Emily was banished for good with plenty of long naps; she was not permitted to get up until dinner time.

And as Emily recounted, "I really wasn't sick, but I had caught a cold and was not myself for a while. So Miss Hayes used my illness as an excuse to get me out of circulation!"

Poor Emily. Deprived of her Chinese heritage! I'm sure if she had been in class we all would have gotten through our first reader quicker!

But when Emily was an adult, she saw Miss Hayes on several occasions and Miss Hayes, who was in her "golden years," apologized to Emily for her strict ways. As Emily put it, "Miss Hayes realized she was unfair!"

And now in the classroom, I kept my head aloft, like a giraffe, to see how the rest of the girls were doing. They were doing fine. It seemed Chinese school was just not for me. Sighing, my eyes wandered across the room and over to the opposite wall where four framed pictures hung over an unused upright piano. These Norman Rockwell pictures of freedom from want, freedom from fear, freedom of speech and freedom to worship made me wonder about these people. They were so different from any people I'd ever seen, with a strong look but weathered and worn and some with comical expressions on their faces. The freedom to worship picture with the old woman's craggy face looked exactly like Miss Hayes' 80-year-old mother, who came to live at the Home. She had her own living quarters with three rooms complete with a kitchen which Miss Hayes had renovated in the back area of the old garage underneath the Lok Hin building. I felt she was lucky as she had everything she needed with so much privacy. We called her Grandma Hayes. Sometimes we'd visit her. I remembered the first time she asked Carol and I if we wanted a cup of tea. We exchanged surprised glances at this question, for after all, tea was reserved only for the teachers at meal time. But it seemed Grandma Hayes was not aware of this! She asked again and we shyly nodded "yes." She seated us around her small dining table. From where I sat I could watch her in the kitchen while she poured the steaming water into her fancy teapot. As we carefully sipped our first taste of her fragrant tea from her fine China we felt like privileged guests. She talked to us, making us feel so special and asked us what we had been doing. Not accustomed to socializing, we responded quickly with one word answers, "playing!"

We adored Grandma Hayes, but after a while we declined the tea, not wanting to bother her because her frail hands trembled and we were afraid she would spill the tea and burn her hands. We also knew we couldn't help her because she wanted to wait on us!

We thought Grandma Hayes was wonderful and wondered why Miss Hayes was so different. But I recalled when Miss Hayes had announced that Grandma Hayes was coming and had encouraged us to visit her mother. And for that I was grateful. But the one thing that stood out in my mind back then and wondered was the unusual coincidence of the two women, they both had hunchbacks!

Now, as an adult, I think they probably had osteoporosis.

And now my gaze shifted from the elderly woman in the freedom picture to the long, narrow, black and white

Chinese scroll with calligraphy hanging next to the chalkboard. It depicted the prodigal sons return and the father's joyous expression. The difference in these pictures fascinated me. Again my eyes moved back to the freedom pictures and a faint smile emerged as I fantasized about a fifth picture titled, Freedom from Chinese School.

Suddenly my daydreams were interrupted by Mrs. Lee's soft voice saying, "All right girls, Chinese school is over!"

I grinned, stood up, push in my chair and said, "Thank you Ley-se-nei."

As the war years continued, Mrs. Lee taught us the Chinese national anthem in Chinese and English and we would sing with zest and vigor.

> *"Arise ye who refuse to be bond slaves*
> *With our very flesh and blood, let us build*
> *our new great wall.*
> *China's masses have met the day of*
> *danger. Indignation fills the hearts of all our*
> *country men. ARISE - ARISE - ARISE,*
> *many hearts with one mind braves the*
> *enemy's gunfire*
> *march on — braves the enemy's gunfire*
> *march on — march on*
> *march on — on."*

Singing this song we felt moved and sang at the top of our lungs! The chorus had a strong marching rhythm and we stood like wooden soldiers and marched in place with arms swinging back and forth. Mrs. Lee smiled broadly. Self consciously, we looked at each other and grinned, sometimes Chinese school was fun!

In 1943, the whole country was buzzing as the wife of the President of China, Madame Chiang Kai - Shek was visiting our country to speak on behalf of the Chinese war effort.

The older girls, from the Ming Quong Home in Oakland, were asked to sing the Chinese national anthem to honor her presence at a special event in San Francisco. Mrs. Lee was extremely excited as she revered Madame Chiang Kai - Shek and thought she was the epitome of an elegant and cultural woman.

The word got back to us that the girls sang each line perfectly and beautifully. Mrs. Lee was very proud. We were thrilled for the older girls and thought they were fortunate to see China's first lady. From the pictures we saw of Madame Chiang Kai - Shek, she was an attractive woman with a pleasant smile. Like Mrs. Lee, Madame Chiang Kai - Shek also dressed in a cheong-saum and her hair was also softly waved and fastened behind her head in a fashionable bun. It seemed Madame Chiang Kai - Shek and Mrs. Lee were from the same aristocratic mold!

After the girls' commanding performance, the exhilarated girls experienced "double-happiness" as they saw the boys from the Chung Mei Home in El Cerrito. Chung Mei was the same type of home as ours except it was for boys. The boys were dressed in their band uniforms in the Chung Mei colors of blue and orange. They had also performed in the same program for Madame Chiang Kai - Shek.

Chung (meaning China) and Mei (America) was also started by the founder of our home, Donaldina Cameron. At that time she also saw a need for a home for Chinese boys. For at the "920" mission, some baby boys were also in her care and she knew that soon they would need another home and a man's influence.

In 1923, Chung Mei, sponsored by the Baptist Church, under the supervision of Dr. Charles R. Sheperd (who later became a friend of Donaldina Cameron), was opened.

**Cousins Nona,
Octavia, Ruby
ca 1942**

The day my sister had arrived at Ming Quong was the time my brother, John, was sent to Chung Mei to live.

Sometime later, I'm not sure when, four of my cousins came to live at Chung Mei and two at Ming Quong. These cousins were the children from my father's oldest sister.

I did not know why my cousins came to the Home, but as an adult, Ellen told me their mother, like our father, had also died of tuberculosis.

My cousins, Octavia and Ruby, had a father who visited them. And one Sunday I was told I had a visitor. I entered the living room and saw my cousins visiting with their father. I was apprehensive. What would this relative be like? He turned in my direction, stopped talking and smiled! I liked him instantly. I finally felt a sense of family.

And now as my mind wandered back to the Oakland girls encounter with the Chung Mei boys, I remembered with happy thoughts the fun day we went on an outing with the Chung Mei boys to Santa Cruz. That day we boarded their personalized bus with their name "Chung Mei" emblazoned on the outside of their gigantic vehicle. For like celebrities, the Chung Mei boys were also paid performers! In 1928, under Dr. Sheperd's leadership, the Chung Mei boys had formed their own band corps and performed in various cities to raise funds for their Home's mortgage.

As we entered their bus, we were timid but quickly became enthralled with the immensity of their bus. What a treat for us to ride in their bus. We felt as if we were on top of the world with a view of the other cars winding along Highway 17. With blue skies above, magnificent mountains and towering redwood trees and a bus load of boys, we were in for a wonderful day!

Amy and I thought a boy named Donald was cute. He sat across from us and we'd get his attention by whispering, "Oooh, Don-ald!" He was very shy and tried to ignore us, but that didn't stop us, we'd just giggle and call his name again. When we debarked at the Santa Cruz boardwalk, lively music from the colorful merry-go-round mixed with the warm air. The spirit of the carnival atmosphere added to our excitement as we strolled, leisurely taking in the amusement rides, the three for ten cent booth games and the view of the pounding surf with the long stretch of beach crowded with sunbathers. With our allowance we could pick a few treasures. My eyes always followed anyone eating the pink cotton candy and inevitably I spent some of my money on the wispy, sweet candy that felt and looked like a cloud!

A few daring girls chose the Giant Dipper. I opted for the safe fun house, while some boys rode the bumper cars and would bump each other with determination. We'd gasp, they'd look at us with shy mischievous smiles, enjoying our attention, and crash some more! Thought we didn't pal around with the boys we definitely sensed their presence. When we passed each other, we'd exchange glances and blush if anyone looked at us too much!

The ocean waves were the most enjoyable part of the day, enjoying the fresh smell of salt. We screamed as the shocking cold water splashed and foamed around our legs and circled our ankles. We didn't wear bathing suits because we were too modest; we only pulled our pedal pushers up to our knees. I always experienced a sensation of the earth pulling away from me and I'd push my toes deeper into the wet sand to maintain my balance. At a distance some boys were swimming in the roaring ocean with another Chung Mei instructor, Lieutenant Tong, a handsome, athletic individual. It was awesome to watch them brave the choppy waves.

I noticed the difference between the boys and us. They were much more adventurous and daring, probably because they were after all "boys" and raised by outgoing men.

At the end of the day, back at the Home, we stood alongside the bus and watched in amazement as Dr. Sheperd expertly maneuvered their bus. As he adjusted himself in the driver's seat he looked at us, tipped his Panama hat, smiled and with one powerful motion of his arm, he pulled the lever and the door "whooshed" shut, and we could feel the gust of air on our sunburned faces. Simultaneously, the bus load of boys and all of us yelled, "Good-bye, Good-bye!" Then Amy and I glimpsed Donald's face turned from us and we hollered, "GOOD-BYE DONALD!" Poor Donald, he blushed profusely. We giggled and waved until their bus was out of sight.

Oh, what fun we had. I think that's when I really started to be interested in boys. I sensed a feeling I was growing up.

My attention came back to the classroom when Jenny nudged me and whispered, "It's almost time to go play." I watched Mrs. Lee straightening her desk top. Finally she looked up and said, "That's all for today girls."

We were so happy to go, we shot up quickly, pushed in our chairs and thanked Ley-sie-nei. We raced to the playground and played on the steel bars and swings. Once outside, the fresh air rejuvenated us.

ca 1937

Fueled with vigor and full of gumption we laughed loudly, "Come on," Jenny cried, "Let's sing our Chinese national anthem."

"Okay," we shouted and with triumphant voices we sang each word clearly and enthusiastically.

We knew Ley-se-nei would have been proud.

And then Jenny yelled, "Hey Nona, say your Chinese name!"

Bernice Wong & Carol Lum

"Um, I can't," I called back, "I can't pronounce it!"
And then I hollered, "You say it!"
"I can't either," Jenny cried.
And everyone laughed — including me!

Chapter 20

Dreamhouse

dreams of yesteryears
weaving fantasies in life
nourishing one's soul...

"Wake up Nona, your dream house is coming up."

"Huh?" I stirred and tried to open my eyes but I couldn't. They felt like they were glued shut. I put my hand up to my face and my fingers felt like frozen popsicle sticks.

Where was I? Why was I so cold? I rubbed my eyelids with my stiff fingers, my face and fingers slowly warmed up. I finally got one eye open and then another, when a sudden gust of wind whipped my hair into my glazed eyes. "Ouch!" I cried out in pain. I held my hair back and looked around and noticed I had an apron on and finally realized where I was. We were riding in the back of Mr. Galeb's open pick up truck. I had dozed off! Mr. Galeb was our boss and we were on our way to his roadside orchards to cut apricots.

At that time I was in the Lok Hin group and I must have been around 11 years old.

It was an overcast morning as the truck sped down the winding roads to Saratoga. We were sitting on wooden fruit boxes, five or six on each side. The cold air was rushing in through the gaps in the side boards causing us to huddle closer for that little bit of extra warmth.

Once again the girls hollered, "Come on Nona, sit up, you're going to miss your dream house." I sat up and turned my head just as we rounded the bend. A massive clump of eucalyptus trees loomed directly above us and through the branches only small patches of sky were visible. Looking up at the towering trees, I always felt very small. It was an awesome feeling. I craned my neck just in time and saw my dreamhouse, almost hidden from view, nestled deeply in the back of a tree lined lot. What a beautiful sight! My eyes, now completely open, took in the English style home. The lush, green lawn, combined with the sudden profusion of magenta bougainvillea spilling over one side of the thatched roof top, left me breathless. The house filled me with the wonderful feeling of being transplanted to England.

Carol nudged me excitedly, "Look at my dreamhouse!" Carol's dreamhouse was a rambling ranch style house with a flat roof. It was tan and trimmed in white. An enormous oak tree framed the house. On the front porch a small collie dog lay sleeping. Devoid of flowers or grass, the barren surroundings matched the house. The stark contrast of her house compared to mine surprised me. Carol's face radiated contentment and I knew how happy she felt. We both sat back with a warm feeling as our dream houses whizzed by.

But once again the cold air circled around us and we crouched down and pulled our sweaters over our heads to cover our windblown hair. While I tried to keep warm, I thought of Miss Hayes following behind us with the station wagon packed with the rest of the Lok Hin and Cottage girls all cozy and warm. But we knew they would have traded places with us in the truck even though we froze in the morning. In the warm evening after work, we enjoyed the cool wind on our tired hot bodies.

Bump, bump, bump, we'd arrived at Mr. Galeb's in Cupertino. As the truck crossed over the railroad tracks we jostled against each other like rag dolls.

Mr. Galeb turned the truck on to the dirt area in front of his one stop family operated grocery store. The lone, country style gas pump was painted deep red and white. As he braked, the truck stopped in a fine cloud of dust which swirled around us and caused us to close our eyes tightly and hold our breath till the dirt died down.

Some girls didn't wait for the dust to settle. They shot up like gazelles and leaped over the sides of the truck. They were so quick they were out even before Mr. Galeb got out of the cab to open the tailgate. They raced over to the open cutting shed, to pick the choice spots for the long day ahead. This shed housed about 12 spots for cutting apricots. The best spots were the ones near the stacked boxes of fruit, so one could see which box of fruit coming up had the largest apricots. The girls who got those boxes finished in half the time that it took those cutting the regular size fruit. The second choice was to check out the trays with the boxes of the biggest fruit available. The boxes were already set up for us at each tray before we arrived. The third pick was to be in the area where the breeze wasthe coolest in the heat of the day. Each box took us about an hour or more to cut and we were paid about 25 cents a box which compared to minimum wage of today (the 1990s) was pretty good pay.

While the girls darted off the truck, I waited for Mr. Galeb's extending hand to help the rest of us off. I was glad he came quickly before all the girls climbed out. I didn't want to be the last one off. That would have been embarrassing, because I wasn't athletic and might be teased because I was afraid I would fall.

As I waited for Mr. Galeb, I could tell by his aggravated expression that he didn't appreciate the girls' enthusiasm. He would have preferred to have them get off at the end of the truck. But he overlooked it. I took Mr. Galeb's supporting hand, stepped down carefully and thanked him. I didn't think he heard me as he barely acknowledged me. He always seemed preoccupied. His day was hectic and full of responsibilities. He was the owner and supervised all the Mexican workers who lived on the premises.

Apricot workers Nona, 2nd from left;
Jenny on right

He was always in a rush, galloping like his name. Mr. Galeb was in his forties, a tall hefty man who seldom talked to any of us. I was intrigued by Mr. Galeb's hair, which was dark brown with massive rings of tight curls. I had never seen hair like this and I couldn't believe someone could have hair so thick and curly. At least his hair wouldn't blow around and whip in his eyes!

My attention moved from his hair to his eyes. I didn't realize he had bent down and was looking at me. Surprised, I jerked back but he told me kindly and matter of factly, "At lunch time go see my wife at the store and she will have a dessert for all of you."

I gasped, "Thank you Mr. Galeb," and ran quickly over to the cutting shed and yelled, "Guess what?"

"What?" the girls hollered back and I blurted out the happy news. "Really?" they asked.

"Yeah," I answered breathlessly, "a dessert!"

"I wonder what we're going to get," mused the girls.

I looked around the shed for my partner Jenny who was one of the girls who had jumped over the side of the truck. I found her at the third choice spot. At least we would be cooled by the breeze.

"Good spot!" I said enthusiastically. She nodded appreciatively.

Our location was next to the only worker Mr. Galeb hired besides us. She was the wife of a Mexican worker. We left this corner spot for her because it was the closest one to her shanty.

This worker who spoke her native language and only broken English kept to herself. Although we greeted her each morning, her face remained expressionless. She appeared bored with life, with all enthusiasm drained from her slovenly body. But she did have a bright little two-year-old daughter, Maria, who was always barefooted and covered with grime from her head to her toes. Her daughter always wore the same tattered dress every day. But underneath all this mess she was the cutest little unkempt girl I've ever seen. Little Maria would wander from the shed constantly during the day and we would hear Maria's mother repeatedly shrieking, "Maria, come back. Come back NOW!"

Poor Maria, she looked so pathetic as she came back and leaned against her mother's ample thighs. Sometimes I would call her over and play just a quick easy game with her because I didn't want to annoy the mother. I would bend way down to Maria's height and put my face in front of her tiny face and "Boo" her. Little Maria's happy squeals made me feel good inside and it also made the working hours fly by.

Every day we shared large wooden slat trays which were the size of a regular size door. Each girl filled their half of the tray with the cut apricots from their own boxes. Miss Hayes had taught us how to grip the apricot in our left hand and with the sharp knife (which she had electrically sharpened the previous night) and with our right hand, we cut from the top of the fruit as we pivoted the fruit with our left hand, so the fruit was cut with one continuous movement. No unevenness or tearing of the fruit was allowed because that produced an inferior product and Mr. Galeb would not be able to get as much money.

When we finished a tray, we would yell, "Tray please!" and one of Mr. Galeb's workers would quickly place another tray on top of the first tray. The same procedure happened when we finished a box of fruit; we yelled, "Fruit please!" The same man came rushing over and carried the heavy box of fruit over to the girl's tray and propped it securely on an empty stand up fruit box. Sometimes we'd have to wait, when the man was busy and as each minute ticked by precious time was being wasted. Once a girl called, "Fruit please!" and the worker was nowhere in sight. She waited and waited. Finally she asked her partner to help her get a box. It was so heavy, they almost dropped it, especially when Miss Hayes' stern voice startled them.

"Girls, you know you're not supposed to get your own fruit." A dreadful silence hung in the air as the girls faces turned red.

Miss Hayes asked, "Why do you think you have a man to help you?"

"But he's not here."

"Answer the question."

"Because we might hurt our backs and maybe damage the fruit!"

"You're right and you both know better than that. Don't ever do that again."

What a relief, they were fortunate this time Miss Hayes only reprimanded them.

Miss Hayes gave us credit for each box completed by punching our tags which were pinned to our aprons. Beverly earned the most money because she was the fastest cutter. Her ticket was always filled with those "enviable holes." Even Miss Hayes cut apricots to help pay for the gas and to keep an eye on us. She also rendered first aid for cut fingers. We knew she enjoyed working with us and was amused by our chatter! She never had to rush like we did. She just cut slowly and leisurely while sitting on a stacked box. We didn't mind Miss Hayes' presence; we were happy and grateful to be able to work and earn our own spending money. We did a good job. Mr. Galeb liked us and each year during the summer vacation we were rehired.

There was one other farmer, Mr. Beamer, whom we worked for several times (after we were done with Mr. Galeb), but we preferred Mr. Galeb and his expertise.

Along with the fruit season the girls from the Ming Quong Oakland home came down to work also. As the girls from our Los Gatos home graduated from the seventh grade, they were generally moved to the Oakland home, so the summer months were fun, because it was reunion time

The girls from Oakland were used to rooming only two to a room, but when they came back here to work, they slept on cots in the laundry's drying room and some camped on cots out on the playground, using the old barn and a large open shed, which was covered on top with palm leaves from our garden. Old bed sheets were tied up from post to post for privacy and wads of newspaper were used to cover holes and keep out the draft. Us younger girls were thrilled at what they had created; for it was just like playing house! But at night, terrible invaders came; bloodthirsty mosquitoes hovered over their sleeping forms and dined on the poor Oakland girls! Once a girl in desperation wrapped her face in cheesecloth, but in the middle of the night she had to go to the bathroom. The sight of this oversized white mummy head terrified the Home's dog and his barking woke up all the tired girls, especially Miss Reber, who of course got the biggest laugh from it.

The Oakland girls were generally driven to other locations to pack cherries and one year, to pick grapes. They later joined us in picking prunes.

The prune season was the most difficult. We wore thick homemade knee pads to protect us from the rocky soil as we knelt to pick the plump purple plums. Each girl had a tin bucket, her empty boxes to fill (which were initialed in chalk by Miss Hayes) and our own row of endless trees, (shaken by the men before we arrived each morning.) And as with apricots, Miss Hayes punched a hole in our tag appropriately for each box of prunes picked. Our pay was about 20 cents per box, which took a little less than an hour to fill.

We were instructed to fill our buckets half-full, so we wouldn't hurt our backs, but as we progressed further along, the distance between the boxes and the trees became too far. So some over-ambitious girls filled their bucket to the top and when Miss Hayes saw that they had disobeyed her orders, she kicked the bucket over, spilling the contents. This frustrated the hard- working girls, but they knew they were in the wrong.

At the end of the working season Miss Hayes totaled our earnings and set aside some money for school clothes. The balance was divided into 12 months. Out of that we contributed one tenth of our earnings to our church (as taught by the Bible). Miss Hayes kept the rest of the money in the office in a separate envelope with our name on it. And it was up to us to keep track of our total. Whenever we needed money for soap, shampoo and other necessities we asked Miss Hayes for it. But we never usually bothered her and would just wait till Saturday when we took our money out for church. Though we earned our own money, we never felt like it was ours, because we never really saw it.

Some girls had families who would send money to them and this was added to their envelope. But for girls like me, there was a special fund if we ran short before the end of the month. This fund was donated by friends of Ming Quong. Although we were aware of this fund, we were not really allowed to use it, because when we did ask for extra money, Miss Hayes needed to know the reason and she never approved of our request. After several attempts to get extra pin money, we gave up. But whatever our request was back then it must have been trivial, for now I cannot recall what they were!

To celebrate the end of the summer season, we all planned a program of songs and skits. Anyone who wanted to participate dolled up with anything they could find out of the ordinary, once even using lipstick and rouge. Some girls borrowed scarves and long skirts from Miss Bergman, who was the tallest teacher at the Home.

Once Bernice Wong wore a gathered skirt and as she danced and pranced across the raised stage (where Carol & I once played house), the usually shy Bernice stopped, turned towards the wall, bumped out her fanny and flipped up her skirt. We were completely surprised. Loud laughter and clapping ensued. We turned to see how the teachers reacted and they were also laughing. Bernice blushed and suppressed a giggle.

After the show, we exclaimed, "Wow Bernice, you did that!"

She laughed, "I had shorts on!"

The head of the Home never said a word, maybe because the Oakland girls were here and the younger girls looked up to them. Or perhaps she knew it was a good outlet for our hard-working days! Whatever the reason, it had been one of the funniest impromptu skits ever performed especially from our sheltered upbringing!

And now, after a few hours of cutting apricots, Jenny called out, "Miss Hayes, what time is it?"

"It's 11 o'clock."

"Oh boy," we enthused, "Only one more hour till lunch time." "Why?" questioned Miss Hayes.

"Because," I piped up, "Mr. Galeb is going to surprise us with dessert."

"Oh." Miss Hayes answered flatly.

How could Miss Hayes forget; we rarely ever got a treat.

Lunch time came along with the high noon. We trekked out to the middle of nowhere, but in the middle of this emptiness were stacks of hay arranged like giant steps; this offered us a slice of shade. Nestled against the fragrant clean straw we plopped down and chomped hungrily on our boring crab-apple jelly sandwich which Miss Reber had labored for days to make, peeling tiny apples from our two crab-apple trees. Miss Reber always said, making crab-apple jelly was going to make her crabby. But of course Miss Reber never was. After I was through with my sandwich, I called out, "Miss Hayes, can we go get the dessert?"

She looked my way and her eyes shifted to the older girls. She singled out a Cottage girl, Bernice Lee, to be the one in charge and told her to pick a helper. Eager cries ran out, "Pick me, pick me!" Bernice picked her sister, Jenny (my partner). Lucky them, I wanted to get the surprise and see the inside of the grocery store. I was disappointed because Mr. Galeb had told me to go see his wife. But I didn't tell that to Miss Hayes, because I knew it wasn't the right thing to do.

We could hardly wait. We watched as Bernice and Jenny walked across the dusty graveled road and entered the store. A few minutes later the door store's screen door opened and Bernice emerged holding a gigantic watermelon.

"Yea! hooray! Watermelon!" we clapped and jumped up and down enthusiastically.

Urging the girls on, we cried, "Hurry! Hurry! Run faster!"

Bernice quickened her pace. And then it happened... Bernice tripped and the watermelon flew out of her arms. We watched in horror as the watermelon cracked and splattered into pieces on the dirt. Chunks of bright red meat strewn the fine dirt and the juicy melon formed little rivulets that quenched the parched ground. We groaned as we surveyed the broken melon. We picked up the larger pieces, some pierced with bits of gravel, and the melon's sweet aroma filled our nostrils. "Miss Hayes, can we wash it off? we called out hopefully.

A stoic Miss Hayes shook her head, "No." Bernice was speechless. Silently we bent down to help Bernice clean up the mess. The sisters walked forlornly back to the store to discard the watermelon. No one spoke, there was nothing to say.

A few minutes later, the screen door swung open again. It was held back by Jenny. And then Bernice emerged holding another watermelon! We couldn't believe it, another one. Mrs. Galeb was so nice.

We were ecstatic; we held our breaths. This time Bernice walked slowly and carefully, cradling the melon like a newborn baby.

Biting into the crispy chunks of sweetness, ice-cold juices ran down our chin, wrist, and forearms. What a mess, but we didn't care. Laughing, we stopped to spit the seeds, trying to out distance the last spitter. Black dots flew like tiddly-winks in all directions leaving soft impressions on the fine dirt.

Mmm, mmm, too bad lunch period had to end.

That evening we all thanked Mr. Galeb and he smiled.

The long ride home with the cool breeze fanning our hot faces felt wonderful. We broke into spontaneous singing and in harmony sang one of our favorite songs,

"There's a long, long trail a-winding into the land of my dreams where the nightingales are singing and my dreams come true..."

As we continued singing I looked into the small back window of Mr. Galeb's truck (where two other girls sat in front also) and could see his smiling profile. He was relaxed too and that gave me a good feeling.

Rounding the bend, Carol's dreamhouse came into view. The collie dog heard us and stood up, wagged its plumed tail, pointed its head upwards and barked along with our singing! We laughed so hard our sides ached. We could see the girls behind us in the station wagon laughing and waving also. Carol's dog was so smart, just like the famous dog Lassie which we saw at the movies.

We approached my dream house and I could see a woman in a white apron holding a spigot can, watering her colorful flowers. She glanced in our direction and I waved and she responded. My heart quickened, my face beamed. Not only was my dreamhouse pretty, but a friendly woman lived there also.

As our dream houses faded away into the distance, I leaned back against the slat-boards and my thoughts drifted to Maria. I could see her sweet face filled mostly with sadness. I thought of her and her family all squeezed into their little shanty and wondered if her parents had their dreams also. Did they dream of a larger house? I wondered if they ever saw the beautiful homes surrounding their outlying area.

A smile crossed my face as I remembered the time Maria's little face lit up when Miss Hayes had let me surprise her with a dress that a Nursery girl had outgrown. But then my smile faded as I recalled her mother's angry face! Poor Maria, her burst of happiness changed to fear, for I unknowingly had hurt the mother's ego, she had lost face! Instinctively I had felt like comforting Maria, but resisted because of her mother's attitude.

I did not understand her mother's reaction. Why couldn't she think of her daughter? How come Maria's mother was like that? Maybe because her life was so mundane, just constant work with nothing to look forward to. Even after work she probably had to cook dinner in their hot one room shanty and Maria would probably be in her way or else wander off causing her mother more grief than happiness. I wondered if they ever played with Maria after dinner. Maybe they went for walks in the evening especially at that time to get away from the fumes of the sulfur house adjacent to their living quarter. The sulfur smoke fumigating the stacks of trays from our cut fruit would cause them to cough and bring on nausea. That used to happen to us when Mr. Galeb used the sulfur house during the day. But that stopped when Miss Hayes talked to him. Now the other poor workers suffered in the evening.

I wish I could take Maria home with us. I would help Miss Chew take care of her and watch over her like a big sister.

My thoughts now shifted to my mother and a sadness filled my heart. I wondered where she was and what she was doing. I wondered how my mother would have reacted. The same way as Maria's mother? I hoped not and I hoped I had not been a burden to her.

Sometimes life could be so sad and so complicated. My thoughts and unanswered questions continued to plague me. But there was one thing I knew I would do when I grew up and lived in my dream house and became a mother. If my child was happy, I too would respond with happiness. From Maria, I had learned the satisfying feeling of giving from the heart. And I knew from my past encounters the warm feelings I received from baby Donnie and now Maria, that children were one of the most precious and wonderful things to hug and to love.

And now as Mr. Galeb's truck approached the Home's open gate, a feeling of deep security filled my entire being; I was home. We could hear the Nursery girl's cheerful welcome, "They're home, they're home." I smiled and thought, not so long ago, I

was that young!

The little ones seemed especially excited tonight and as they clustered around us, they cried, "We get to eat outside tonight."

Just then, a wonderful aroma drifted from the kitchen; Miss Reber was creating again and I was hungry.

"Come on," the young ones cried. "Come see."

We all ran over to the side of a slight slope and peered over at the large wood deck surrounding a 500-year-old oak tree and we could see the outdoor tables set for dinner.

What a treat. We were so fortunate...it felt so good to

be home.

Looking back, life for me at the Home was good. But a few of the other girls, whom I've kept in contact with, see the Home differently. They feel no connection with the Home (except for the girls). As Paula put it, "Nona, I didn't know you liked the Home that much!"

I had adjusted. I felt secure. I couldn't imagine another type of life. If I had lived with my relatives, life would have been the complete opposite.

Stories from Ellen (my half-sister) were the type similar to some of the girls Donaldina Cameron had rescued.

As Ellen related, when her mother died, our father remarried (my mother). Ellen then moved in with the grandparents. Grandma was an authoritarian figure with a cruel streak. Because she had no love in her heart for Ellen, she utilized an age-old Chinese belief to extremes, that the boys in the family were priceless and that girls were of no value (the adult females gained some respect after marriage, especially if they bore sons).

Every day, Ellen did all the cooking for both my mother and grandmother's household. In grandma's house that included five children and all of grandpa's hungry farm workers. She also did all the household chores, which in those days included chopping wood each morning (before anyone else was awake) for the stove, which also served as the only heating system in the house. In the evening she shared a bed with an aunt. Many times, depending on the aunt's mood, she would kick

Ellen out of bed. Ellen spent many nights on the hard floor. (Ellen was older than her aunts and uncles, because

grandma came to this country after Ellen was born.)

Mental abuse was also used by grandma, who constantly compared her daughter to Ellen, telling Ellen that she was ugly Ellen learned not to complain, for if she did, she was kicked, hit or whipped by grandma and on several occasions struck by her stepmother (my mother).

Our father, (who had come to America with grandpa at around 9 years of age) never interceded on Ellen's behalf, for he was out working and besides, it was grandma (his mother) who ruled the household.

As for grandpa, he too was working out in the vegetable fields and did not see all the hardships she endured, although sometimes when he was around and saw her hard at work, he said nothing. Even though grandpa was the kindest person in the household, he went along with whatever grandma said.

Ellen had no one to confide in, even when grandpa's farm workers deprived of their wives in China, molested her.

In order to cope, she escaped to her knitting. School was also another safe place where she could rest and find refuge.

But one time, this backfired on her. Exhausted and sleepy, Ellen dozed off in the classroom. After school, the teacher questioned her about this but Ellen only told her that she worked hard. So, that one day Ellen was late coming home, grandma was waiting with the whip!

And as Ellen said, "In those days I didn't know about child welfare."

Why Ellen was not sent to the Home is not known. Maybe because she was so much older than me (13 years) or maybe because she was from a different mother.

Ellen had two aunts, Sara and Yute (her mother's sisters) who at that time lived at the Ming Quong Home adjacent to Mills College. Her aunts tried to get Ellen into the Home, but when grandma heard about it, she said, "No," and then told Ellen that Ming Quong was a terrible place to live and they mistreated the girls. By then, Ellen had no desire to go to the Home and she felt sorry for us.

Looking back, Ellen realized grandma had lied and needed to keep her at the farm to be her slave. Ellen's life was not a typical Chinese upbringing. For even though girls were not as important to the family, there was still love between a parent and a daughter.

What a life my poor sister had. I'm sure if I had been raised like her, I probably would not have survived.

Chapter 21

Escape into trouble

books are wonderful friends
expanding one's soul to flight
intermingling minds

At the school's spacious library, each class was privileged to use the library once a week. At that time, I was 11 years old and in the sixth grade. My favorite book was Heidi. She was an adorable orphan with black curly hair. She lived with her kind gray-haired grandpa in the Swiss Alps. I was completely entranced with the book's illustrations and a story similar to mine. I checked out the book repeatedly and would daydream of Heidi's idyllic life with a grandpa who loved her. I could feel their special love for each other and wished I could be like Heidi, surrounded with love, hugs and kisses.

But then one day the book was not in its usual spot and the same thing happened the following week. I became apprehensive and confused. What happened to the book?

At first, I wondered if I should ask the librarian. I was a little scared of her strict attitude, and besides I didn't want to bother her. But I missed Heidi so much, I made up my mind I wasn't going to be afraid and quickly walked up to the librarian's desk. "Excuse me, but could you please tell me where "Heidi" is, I can't find it on the shelf."

The librarian looked at me blankly as if she didn't understand my question. Then she repeated, "Heidi?"

"Yes," I answered timidly.

"Oh yes, I remember now, that book has been discarded."

"But why?" I cried.

"Because the book was no longer serviceable, it was old and tattered."

I was devastated and speechless and just stared blankly at the librarian.

She returned my silent look with an expression of, "Can't you understand that?"

But I just stood there as if grounded to the floor and in an attempt to appease me said, "There are plenty of other books you can read."

But I didn't care about the other books.

She didn't understand. Completely frustrated, all I could think about was Heidi and how someone had thrown out a book that was so meaningful.

I felt a part of me had been discarded also. Now I could no longer turn the pages and read into it all the things I missed from my own life. Because at the Home there was never any display of love or affection. I wondered how it felt to be hugged. And I thought it really must be a nice feeling to be able to cuddle in Grandpa's arms and then put my arms around him and shower him with my love and adoration and just smile into his kind face. After that I didn't really care to go to the library. It was too frustrating. I spent the entire period wandering up and down the aisles skimming through rows and rows of books trying to find another meaningful book. I thought there would be no other book in the world like Heidi.

But one day I saw a book lying on the library table and its title intrigued me, White Fang by Jack London. "What was a white fang?" I wondered. I opened the book and was enthralled. White Fang was a lone wolf who survived many life threatening obstacles. No matter what hardship he encountered like long wintry days without food, or being attacked by an enemy, he didn't falter for he knew instinctively he could make it. I liked that and felt an identity. My private mourning was over. I devoured all books pertaining to courageous animals, whether it was a horse, a dog or a bear. It made no difference, they just all had to have one thing in common, the spirit of White Fang.

Back at the Home, in the corner of the playroom, was a small built-in bookcase with three shelves. The doors were beveled glass and one could see right away what book was available, which wasn't much as the shelves were usually empty. But the Home did have a popular series of Nancy Drew mystery books and we all anxiously waited our turn to read them. I loved each one.

One day, Beverly and I were thumbing through the books grumbling, "There's nothing good to read."

Beverly and I were good friends, because not only were we classmates in school, but we had this deep interest in reading.

But there was one thing that bothered me about Beverly. While she was absorbed in her books she had a habit of using her fingers to twist and roll her lower lip. It looked unsightly and disfiguring. Beverly was such a tomboy, she never gave a second thought to her appearance.

Top row left, Beverly, Nona (next to her good friend Betty) Bottom row left, Karl and Marianne

I tried to tell her, "It looks ugly when you twist your lips, why don't you stop."

"Huh?" she said, as she looked up from her book. I repeated my statement and added, "What if it stayed that way?"

"Oh," she replied and continued her reading. And once again Beverly absentmindedly began to twist her lips. I gave up and sighed, "Oh well, that's Beverly."

And now I said to Beverly, "Let's do something different." "What?" she implored.

"Let's go outside and play Robin Hood."

Beverly was silent, but I knew she was thinking, "What would we use for a bow and arrow?"

"Yeah, you're right," I answered.

Then I brightened, "How about playing the bandit of Sherwood Forest and you can be Cornel Wilde?"

Beverly and I thought the handsome movie actor, Cornel Wilde, was so dashing in the movie. I liked his smile, his confidence and how he was the underdog but always came out ahead. He was my dream man. But as with the first suggestion, this time we had no swords.

At the Home, there was never any pictures on any of the bedroom walls, only in the main building. But if we could, I would have put up Cornel Wilde.

Walking by the Lok Hin building, I spied a discarded brown rope on the floor of the old garage and hollered, "Hey Beverly, look, a rope. Let's play Tarzan and Jane."

And off we went looking for the perfect tree to swing from. We found one, but it was too tall and the second tree, though smaller, was still too high for us to loop the rope over, even the lowest branch. We looked for the gardener for help, but he was nowhere in sight. Disappointed, we knew we had to look for a smaller tree, even though it wouldn't be much fun. Approaching the new aluminum garage, which was adjacent to a slight embankment, we saw a young pepper tree on the bank, which was ideal, because it made the tree appear taller. With renewed energy we managed to snag a branch.

Beverly climbed the tree and we were finally ready. Observing Beverly from her lofty height, she grinned down at me triumphantly as she clung to the rope and flew through the air, just the way Tarzan did in the comic books. She then let out the famous Tarzan cry, "Aie-eeii-Aiee-eeii!"

I doubled over with laughter and wished I was brave like her and had the courage to swing off a tree.

And then it happened — the rope broke. Beverly came tumbling down along with the branch full of pink little peppercorns. Debris flew in all directions. The warm air was spiced with dust and pepper. In shock, I ran the short distance and knelt down next to Beverly's crumpled form. She didn't move.

"Beverly," I cried, "Are you all right?" She moaned. Frantically, I cried again, "Beverly, are you all right?" She stirred and I felt relieved. Only moving one arm, Beverly attempted to right herself. I helped her up and her hand shot over to her stomach.

"It hurts," she winced.

"Oh, Beverly, we better go tell a teacher."

"No," she said weakly as she straightened up and brushed off her overalls. I bent over to pick up the rope. It was so frayed. We had no idea the rope was so weak. "It's a good thing," I thought, "that the tree was on that bank because the ground was higher."

Poor Beverly. I asked again, "Don't you think you should see a teacher?"

"No, I'm all right now. It doesn't hurt any more." I knew Beverly was in pain, but I also knew she would be in big trouble if we got caught swinging off a tree.

Suddenly a voice rang out, "Beverly, Nona. Miss Hayes wants to talk to you."

Petrified, we gasped, "Miss Hayes wants to talk to us!

How does she know?" We thought no one had seen us. Our eyes quickly darted around the yard. No one was around. The voice came closer, "Nona and Beverly, where are you?" the voice demanded, "Miss Hayes wants to talk to you."

"What shall we do with the rope," we whispered. Looking around we saw a low bush and with a flurry we kicked the rope under the bush.

Gaining our composure we cried, "We're coming." We walked quickly up the driveway to the office. As we approached the girl we asked, "What does Miss Hayes want?"

"I don't know, but she looked mad."

"Uh-oh, don't say anything Beverly," I reminded her as I hurriedly brushed off any lingering debris.

"I won't," said Beverly, "No one saw us anyway." Once more I asked, "Does it still hurt?"

"No," she answered emphatically. This time I believed her. Apprehensively, we knocked at the office door.

"Come in," said Miss Hayes. Miss Hayes was seated at her rolled up top desk. She turned and we saw a face locked in anger. With an exaggerated jerk, she opened the lower drawers and took out two magazines — a Tarzan comic book and a movie magazine. Our faces flushed, we were stunned.

She demanded, "Are these yours?"

Like mutes we stared blankly at each other and barely nodded, "Yes, Miss Hayes."

I wondered how she knew. How did she find them? Who had told on us? Did someone see us secretly reading in the garden? We had always been so careful. Whenever we heard anyone approaching we'd duck for cover or creep out silently and escape to another corner of the garden. But now, Miss Hayes had gone through our belongings and found them. We thought we had been so clever tucking them under our mattresses.

With my gaze fixed on the movie magazine, I realized why Miss Hayes had rummaged through our belongings. Months ago the Home was filled with excitement as I had received a letter from the child actress, Connie Marshall. We had seen a heartwarming movie, starring Walter Brennan and her. Touched by the story and her performance, I wrote her, conveying my feelings and also told her about my life at the Home. Her address had been in the magazine.

Miss Hayes had been upset about my letter to Connie Marshall. She interrogated me repeatedly, "What did you tell her about the Home? What did you say?" In all innocence, I replied, "Nothing, just what we do everyday, like go to school, do our work, go to church, just things like that." "Are you sure, you told nothing else?" "No," I replied.

Anyway, it was weeks before I could get the letter. She had no alternative but to give it to me as an older girl had been assigned to pick up the mail and when she saw a bright red, small envelope from Twentieth Century Fox, everyone knew. I was in such an exhilarated state, I daringly slipped into the office, not once, but twice and looked at the handwritten letter addressed to "Nona Mock." I was so excited and frustrated because I wanted to open it. When I finally was given the letter, I read it over and over. Connie had also told me about her life and how she planned to send me an 8x10 autographed picture of herself under separate cover. I wondered what separate cover meant, but I never found out because I never received the picture! From then on, only the teachers picked up the mail.

Now looking at Miss Hayes' irate expression, her snapping voice continued, "Where did you get the magazines?"

"From the Drug Store," we stammered.

"Oh, from the Drug Store," she mimicked sarcastically. "And how did you get them? You know you're forbidden to buy comic books and magazines." Before we could answer she rampaged on, "And where did you get the money?" We looked at the floor. "I'm waiting for your answer," she stormed, "and look at me when I talk to you!"

We looked up into Miss Hayes' piercing gray eyes and she glowered, "And tell the truth!"

"We took them."

"You what? You took them?" "Yes."

"Why?"

"Because we didn't have any money and we wanted to read them."

"But that's stealing!" she blurted. We looked at her uncomfortably and nodded.

She seethed with anger and it seemed invisible fumes flared from her nostrils as she muttered under her breath. She opened the drawer again and pulled out a glamour girl fold out card. I gasped silently and felt a rising heat enveloping my face. Even Beverly hadn't known about this card.

Miss Hayes glared at me and I mumbled, "I took that from a Cigar and Candy store." We looked at each other while Miss Hayes exploded into a tirade of how bad we were and how she was going to punish us. In exasperation she could see we were not afraid of her. With her flashing eyes she spewed forth, "You two are to take the magazines back to the store, apologize to the owners, and pay for the magazines from your allowance! Do you understand?"

"Yes, Miss Hayes."

The next day after school, Beverly and I stopped at the Cigar and Candy store. Beverly waited outside. With great trepidation I walked in alone because Miss Hayes had said, "I had to face the owner myself." The store was small and rarely busy. The owner, a wiry man in his forties, with slicked back hair, looked down at me from behind his raised counter and asked, "Do you want something?" Self consciously I held out the card and uttered, "I'm sorry I took this," and handed it back to him along with the money.

Frowning, he asked, "What's this money for?"

"I have to pay for it."

He was taken back and held back a laugh. With a wry grin he took the card and money and nodded. I left hurriedly.

Beverly asked, "What did he say?"

"Nothing! I was so embarrassed. I thought he was going to laugh at me."

Beverly made no reply. We continued on to the Drug Store. The outside of the store was lined on both sides with an abundance of interesting magazines. We wanted to read all of them.

We asked for the owner and watched a harried man walk rapidly towards us. He was dressed in a white pharmaceutical jacket.

We told him why we were there and he took us to his back room with no windows. The room was so small there was barely enough room for his wooden desk and chair. A single light bulb hung from the ceiling. It cast a disarming glow on the paneled walls. It was stifling and confining.

He listened to our confession. With exasperation, he took the magazines and threw them on his desk and pocketed the money. With rapid fire he threatened to take us across the street to the Police Department. Sputtering on he thundered, "Maybe they'll put you two in jail. Would you like that?"

Terrified, we answered, "No." He glowered at us. We left the store shaken with his loud threats still ringing in our ears.

"Whew, he was sure mean and different from the other man," I said.

"Wow, what if we had to go to the Police!" We walked home in silence. Miss Hayes had punished us well.

A few weeks later, while dressing for school, my excitement began to mount for it was the sixth grade picnic at the park. I wore my favorite one piece blue and white outfit. It was special as it was shorts but looked like a dress.

Our school teacher, Mrs. Campbell, summoned Beverly and I up to her desk. She told us coldly that Miss Hayes had called and told her that we were not to go to the class picnic because Miss Hayes was still punishing us.

I was crushed, but Beverly wasn't. Embarrassed and self- conscious, I wondered if our teacher knew what we did.

Mrs. Campbell placed us under another teacher's care. We stayed behind on the playground as our classmates took off to the park. I sadly watched them leave. Each happy student was holding a jar, for scooping polliwogs out of the creek. One student turned and yelled cheerfully, "Come on Chief!" Chief loped behind them with his tail flopping from side to side. We didn't want to play with anyone so Beverly and I took off by ourselves.

"What shall we do?" I grumbled. "Let's play hopscotch."

"No."

"How about tetherball?"

"No."

As we drifted aimlessly around the grounds, my eyes landed on a penny. "A penny, Beverly!" I cried. We ran around quickly and found another penny. We were happy hunting. I had forgotten that on the school grounds, if you had nothing else to do, one could always look and usually find a penny or two. With the pennies in our pockets, we were laughing and I almost forgot the picnic.

"Hey, let's buy some candy after school," I suggested.

"Okay," Beverly agreed.

So after school, Beverly walked in alone to the Cigar and Candy store. I lagged behind anxiously. I didn't want the cigar man to see me! When Beverly emerged she was smiling broadly.

"What did you buy?" I cried.

"A Tootsie Roll and a Blackjack."

"Oh boy, mmm, mmm." We split the secret sweets and headed home.

And to this day, Beverly still has the childhood scar on her stomach, which occasionally pains her.

And what did we learn that day? I'm not sure, but unpleasant things like that are remembered forever!

But as Amy recently reminded me, we did have movie magazines at the Home, because we use to cut out our favorite movie stars and paste them in our scrapbooks. I then recalled my scrapbook and remembered how we would trade pictures with each other. Back then I also adored little Margaret O'Brien and my scrapbook was filled with her pictures, especially when she starred in the movie, Journey for Margaret.

It would seem Miss Hayes gave into our preteen fantasies (after what Beverly and I did!) and permitted us to spend our allowance on movie magazines. Maybe back then, that was what I asked for in pin money and was denied!

As for the lack of affection from the teachers at the Home, I felt that happened because of institutional living. The teachers may have wanted to hug us, but because there were so many girls around, if they hugged one girl and not another, I'm certain there would have been tension. I think their formula was to keep it simple.

Yet, Rhoda thought differently. She felt it was because of the lack of affections shown the teachers in their upbringing which resulted in the same upbringing for us. But, as Rhoda said, "They nurtured us in other ways, they provided us with our physical needs, that was their love. As we grew we learned by observing the many types of love."

As I listened to Rhoda's theory I recalled when I saw my first kiss between a man and a woman. I was probably around 11 years old. There was a new, young teacher, Miss Carmichael, who worked at the Ming Quong Home in Oakland. For some reason, she had come down to the Los Gatos Home for the day. Her fiancée, who was attending Stanford's Medical School, was to pick her up later in the afternoon.

During the day, there was excited talks amongst us girls that the two of them were in love. We waited in anticipation for his arrival because we'd never seen anyone in love.

When his coupe drove up the driveway, Miss Carmichael came sprinting out the front door, right into his opened arms. From the sidelines, we discreetly watched them embrace and kiss. They had looked tenderly into each others eyes and we could see the love between them.

At that time, I also noticed Miss Carmichael's blushing face.

Silent "Ooooo's" had gushed from us as we looked at each other and giggled in delight.

Chapter 22

First Period

manifestation
womanhood blossoms with change
period is life

One breezeless summer night after dinner, the Cottage girls called to us from the playground, "Who wants to play Old Mother Witch?"

"We do, we do," the younger ones hollered and the whole play yard chimed in also because we loved to play with the older girls and old mother witch was one of our favorite games. We all ran to the outside stairs of the Lok Hin building.

Lok Hin Building

A Cottage girl, named Bessie, was singled out to play the witch. Bessie's nickname was Boots because she resembled the popular cartoon character, Betty Boop; with her enormous eyes and thick wavy hair. Her nickname also meant "passing gas", the Chinese slang for "fong pei", of which she was famous for! But everyone liked Boots because of her good nature.

"Listen," she yelled, "when you start calling "Old Mother Witch," I will get mad and chase you around this large circle and if I catch you, I'll lock you up over there," she explained, pointing to the stairs. "Everyone understand?" Little heads bobbed up and down in acknowledgment. She slowly rolled her eyes around the circle, with her arms raised above head she hollered, "Ready?"

"Ready!" we shouted.

"Go," yelled Witchy Boots as she glared at us.

In our sing song voices we taunted, "Old Mother Witch/who went to the ditch/picked up a penny/and thought she was rich."

We huddled together in pretend fright. She wasn't mad, so we raised our voices, and chanted again, "Old Mother Witch/who went to the ditch/picked up a penny..." When all of a sudden she sprang at us. Our hearts jumped and with loud screams we scattered down the sloped circle as she ran after us. Boot's hands reached out and snatched a screaming girl.

"Gotcha!" she cackled. Shrieking with laughter we all stopped and stayed in place, as she pulled the reluctant girl back to the stairs and in a make belief gesture locked her up. Our bodies were tense and ready to start playing again when we heard Mrs. Lee's soft voice, "Lok Hin girls come in! Tonight is darning night!"

We moaned. We'd completely forgotten. Once a week after our prayer time we had to go to Mrs. Lee's bedroom to darn our socks.

"Come, hurry girls," Mrs. Lee's urgent voice continued.

We reluctantly stopped. One younger girls wailed pitifully, "It won't be fun now without the Lok Hin girls."

We looked at Mrs. Lee, hoping she'd let us off but she continued walking up the stairs to her room.

Disappointed we yelled to the others, "Maybe we can darn fast."

Miss Bergman, Miss Davies,
Miss Reber, Miss Hayes

"Okay, hurry!" yelled the Witch.

We ran up the stairs and charged into our bedroom; rummaged through our drawers and took out all our socks. We grabbed our chairs and filed into Mrs. Lee's bedroom. We quickly dragged our chairs around in a circle and we were ready. This was the time Mrs. Lee would sometimes talk to us about being Chinese, and how the other teachers (because they were Caucasian) might not understand us, but we could always ask her anything. I'd look at her and wonder what she meant. The other teachers never gave us any reason to ask Mrs. Lee questions. Mrs. Lee always seemed to anticipate something that never happened. I didn't see anything different about being Chinese, especially living in a household of all Chinese girls. But of course at school we stood out with our jet black hair and rice- bowl haircuts. We didn't think about our facial features being different from our classmates because no one called it to our attention. From the students there were no name calling one might associate with minorities. We were accepted in the upscale town of Los Gatos.

At that time, Ming Quong was the only institution in

the United States that admitted Chinese girls. Most institutions had strict rules forbidding the practice. It was also the only institution that had long term care. So Mrs. Lee as an adult may have sensed or experienced different responses. But her remark about the teachers not understanding us was a definite puzzle to me.

Sunshine Cottage, left; house
on right acquired later

The first 10 girls who came to the Home in 1934 and lived in a two bedroom house on Loma Alta Avenue called Sunshine Cottage under the supervision of Miss Bankes and Miss Callecod may have bridged the way for us and may have had to overcome prejudice. But from my experience the community of Los Gatos was made up of well-educated, self-confident people who only saw us as individuals in need of our type of home.

Growing up, our main concern about being Chinese meant we had to go to Chinese school. But because of Chinese school we stood out! Karl asked Beverly and I and another girl in our class from the Home to autograph the back of his school picture along with our Chinese names. We were surprised. It was fun and I was filled with pride. All the years of Chinese School were not in vain! But I remembered I was envious of my classmates with their big, black and white picture, because I didn't have one, for the Home simply had no money for pictures; it would have been an unnecessary expense.

And just recently, Karl Schwarz, my elementary classmate, related that he thought the girls from the Ming Quong Home were amazing, because we could speak Chinese and anyone who could write Chinese the way we did had to be smart. I was so surprised to hear that for Karl had actually been envious of us back then! And at that time he also thought we were exotic! His desire back then, (along with his classmates) was to be invited up to the Home for a visit and to eat Chinese food, because that had been the talk! Karl's memories jogged mine and I remembered we had wanted them to come up, but I don't remember if we asked the teachers as they had enough to do. Besides, I'm sure the answer would have been, "No!" For we simply didn't socialize at the Home.

In the classroom at school, I do remember the difference of one girl, Marianne Swanson, who sat in front of me. And all I could see was this cloud of fine blond hair. It was incredibly fantastic. Marianne had a comb and when the teacher was busy at the chalkboard, I combed the back of her hair till it was smooth as silk. It was incredibly beautiful. I wondered why she didn't comb her hair more often, because her hair when combed looked like spun gold.

But one source of difference which I never talked to Mrs. Lee about was our annual picnic at the downtown park, next to the town's only swimming pool.

This celebration was either for the Fourth of July or Labor Day, and it was an extra exciting day because it was a time for everyone at the Home to relax and have fun.

At these picnics we bundled up yummy bologna sandwiches (not jam) and for this occasion Miss Reber also made her delicious macaroni salad and off we went to the swimming pool. Each girl was responsible for carrying their own bathing suit and cap which we rolled up securely in our towel and tucked under one arm.

The carload of teachers would follow shortly with the food and paper plates and other supplies. We would always try to outrace the teachers to the pool, but of course after a short while, we would hear the honking of the horn behind us and see Miss Reber's smiling face, which made us laugh and we'd wave and tingle with more excitement as we ran faster.

Each year we ran all the way to the pool!

We would arrive out of breath and dripping with perspiration and catching our breath we'd look around. And what we saw always amazed us, because it seemed the entire population of Los Gatos was there, for every square inch of the park was filled.

The teachers took care of securing enough picnic tables while we headed to the pool. This was our chance to show our swimming skills to the teachers who would be relaxing on the spectator's bench and watching us from behind the cyclone fence.

A Cottage girl in charge of the younger girls paid the entrance fee for all of us. The checker would count all our happy faces and total up the amount. And then she would ask her usual question, "Do you need towels?" We'd look at each other and grin. Couldn't she see our towels?

The older girl, replied, "No, we have our own towels." And I would wonder why the other people didn't bring their towels. Did they forget? I didn't realize then what a luxury it was.

We changed in a flash for it was easy to put on our one-piece bathing suits with no ties. Our suits were plain and not decorative or colorful as most of the other swimmers in their two-piece swimsuits, but we didn't really care. All we cared about was swimming. But before we reached the open door leading to the pool, we all had to pass under a shower of cold water (as was the rules of the pool). The shock of cold water on our hot bodies brought piercing screams and squeals which echoed throughout the building and could be heard by the concerned lifeguards and even the teachers who were at the other end of the pool. Everyone knew the Ming Quong girls were about to emerge!

We came out oblivious of our noise and quickly walked to the shallow end, remembering the rules of the pool, "no running." To be reprimanded by the lifeguard would be the most embarrassing thing.

Some girls jumped in, while others like me stepped down gingerly, holding on to the handrail. We cavorted like dolphins, swimming, splashing, and submerging ourselves to see who could stay underwater the longest.

After a while the pool became so crowded we couldn't even move more than one stroke at a time. So the lifeguard had to announce that five minute intervals were allowed for a certain age group. And after the time had elapsed he blew his whistle for the next group. That was more fun. That enabled us to at least stroke about four times before we bumped into another swimmer.

After our swim we looked forward to our special lunch. But the next episode before we started to eat was not fun. It was a point of complete humiliation, for the head of the home announced out loud for everyone to hear, (even those at the nearby tables) that instead of a teacher saying a prayer, we were all to sing, "Break thou the bread of life..." Of course all heads turned in our direction. And when we sang, strangers whom we had never even seen in either school or church stopped talking or playing and stared at us as we all bowed our heads and closed our eyes. I felt those stares barreling into me. My face was flushed, I wished I wasn't there. I felt the other picnickers thought we were weird.

Now this repeated, humiliating experience I'm sure was not what Mrs. Lee meant! But if I had talked to her about it, could she have prevented this from occurring? I doubt it, for I felt the head of the home sensed our embarrassment and it was her way to let us know who was in charge and she also wanted everyone around to know what a good job she was doing in raising us and how we were such good obedient Christian girls!

And we were! We never talked back or argued with the teachers. Just like when Mrs. Lee called us now for our darning lesson we just obeyed for that was the way of the Home.

So tonight as we settled down I noticed Mrs. Lee seemed a little flustered. I wondered why. Maybe this time there would be no singing, which would be unusual for she always taught us the Lok Hin song which she had composed. It had a short catchy melody and as we mended our socks weaving our needle up and down across the soft triple thread to the rhythm of our song. Our song was woven not only in memory but in our socks as well! Just like our singing in Chinese school made Mrs. Lee happy, the singing of her Lok Hin song doubled her happiness as she sang along with us.

We are little joy givers of Ming Quong / in our work and in our play / you can hear our songs / songs of everlasting joy / brightening up the day / happy, happy we are here / for our hearts are gay.

Mrs. Lee had a way of making our work lighter and we felt special having our own song. She never made up songs for the other groups, although she did give a Chinese name to the Nursery and the Starlight groups. The Nursery group was called Fook Yow meaning, we receive blessing from childhood. The Starlights were named Ching Sum meaning Pure Heart.

Now as we looked at Mrs. Lee's nervous face, she cleared her throat and said timidly, "Girls, tonight I have something important to tell you."

And her face turned red; she was blushing. I was right. Something different was going to happen, there would be no singing tonight! She sat demurely and was smoothing her Chinese dress over her tiny lap. We waited as she again cleared her throat and repeated, "Girls I have something to tell you about your body...when..." she hesitated.

We asked, "What is it, Mrs. Lee?"

The Starlight group

"When you get older your body will change."

"What do you mean, Mrs. Lee?"

We looked at each other and smiled mischievously. We knew bodies change and women developed a figure, and we all knew Miss Davies had a big bosom ("top" as we called it). And Miss Higgins' (the head of the Home in Oakland) top was so big and broad that it reminded me of a convenient built-in tray!

When I was around 8 years old and in the Starlight group, I was curious about the adult body and because Miss Davies had the biggest top I'd ever seen I wondered what it looked like. On the Starlight sleeping porch my bed was underneath her bedroom window and at night a thin stream of light shown under her curtains. I thought if I could peek in I could see her top.

One time, late at night, I heard Miss Davies getting ready for bed. I looked around the dark porch and it seemed everyone was sound asleep. This was my chance and I thought, "Should I? or shouldn't I?" Though my heart was pounding, I took the chance and got up slowly and peeked under the curtain. My body was tense, a girl stirred and I stiffened but she continued breathing soundly. I could see Miss Davies' back, she was facing her open closet door. She had her bathrobe draped over her shoulders and was undressing with her robe on! What a disappointment. Now I had to wait another night!

Miss Davies, Miss Reber, Miss Chew

The next night it was the same thing. I saw nothing! I was so tired and sleepy from waiting that when my head hit my mattress I fell asleep almost instantly, but not before the question entered my mind, "Why did Miss Davies undress that way? Maybe because she had been a missionary and was really modest. But that was probably just the way she undressed.

And now as I looked at Mrs. Lee her face turned a deeper shade of crimson and she proceeded, "Once a month you will bleed!"

"Bleed? What do you mean?" we questioned. We stopped our darning and gave her our undivided attention.

"It will not hurt you. You will bleed down here," and she pointed to her crotch.

Our eyes widened and questions poured forth from us, "Bleed down there?" we asked aghast, "Are you sure it won't hurt us?" "Why do we bleed?" we asked in horror.

"Because you are growing up."

We looked at each other blankly. I didn't understand what Mrs. Lee was saying.

"When you bleed it's very little and it won't hurt much." "I thought you said it wouldn't hurt?"

"Well sometimes your stomach might hurt a little but it will be alright." As she talked she opened a brown paper bag on the floor next to her and took out a blue and white box labeled Kotex and pulled out a soft white gauzy pad.

"Now girls, this is what you wear when you bleed."

Now I finally knew why two Cottage girls were carrying boxes of these up to Mrs. Lee's room. I wondered what they were and asked, "What's in those boxes?"

A Cottage girl answered evasively, "It's for Mrs. Lee." "Are they Kleenex?"

"No," she answered sharply.

So I stopped my questioning. The girls were unloading them from a shiny black limousine. The owner of the car was a tall, friendly Chinese man, who was Mrs. Lee's friend and he was also a relative of a Lok Hin girl, Mary Jane. He was the manager for the National Dollar store in San Jose and he would deliver these boxes frequently. Now I at last knew the secret, they were for bleeding!

The girls continued, "How do you wear the pad, Mrs. Lee.?" From her bag this time she took out a strange narrow elastic belt with two dangling flat silver hooks. She asked a girl to stand up and with her help, she had the girl step into the belt and pulled it up to the waist and hooked both ends of the pad to the hooks.

The self conscious girl looked down and made a face.

Mrs. Lee explained, "You wear this underneath your pants." It looked strange. "How does it feel?" we asked.

"Funny," she blushed.

"Try walking!" we cried. She did and the belt and pad stayed securely in place.

Mrs. Lee said, "Now girls I want all of you to try it on!" We took turns while girls giggled nervously. It felt peculiar.

"And girls when a pad is used you wrap it in newspaper and throw it away."

"How do you know when you will start bleeding?"

"You don't know but most girls start between ten to thirteen years old or later."

We looked at each other and realized we were in that age group. It could be any day!

"Does this happen to you, Mrs. Lee?"

Mrs. Lee hesitated, but answered quickly, "Yes." We looked at her in astonishment.

"Why do you bleed, Mrs. Lee?"

"Because I'm a lady and a mother. Soon you too will grow up and you will have to act more ladylike, and not climb trees and act like tomboys." Tomboys! That must mean daring Edna who was so rough and tumble. We always called her a tomboy.

Then I recalled seeing Edna in the kitchen not once but twice surrounded by two older girls and Miss Reber's amused face! I wondered why Miss Reber was smiling. I looked again and it seemed Miss Reber thought Edna was exaggerating. Edna was acting strangely. She was sitting on a stool and was completely bent over, resting her head on the kitchen table clutching her stomach and moaning loudly. She sounded bad, like she should be in the infirmary. On the table next to her was a mug of hot water to soothe her pain. I called in the first time and asked Miss Reber, "What's the matter with Edna?"

Miss Reber casually remarked, "She has a stomach ache. Go on now, go outside and play and leave Edna alone."

"Strange," I thought, no one with a stomach ache ever acted like that. The older girls were trying to comfort Edna. I ran out to play but my mind could still see Edna's agonizing face and I wondered the second time I saw her in pain Edna must really be hurting because she was such a tomboy hardly anything ever hurt her. "Could this be connected with bleeding?" I thought. If not, she should be in the infirmary where Miss Davies, who was in charge of sick girls, would keep her in bed for at least three days till her daily morning temperature registered a normal 98.6 degrees. While there, she would be separated from any of the girls who might be isolated in separate rooms with contagious diseases, like the measles or mumps. And no matter how restless Edna became she could not visit with the isolated girls, because of what happened one night. After the girls knew the teacher was through checking them for the night, one group of girls decided to visit the other girls. They had a great time visiting, but of course they all ended up with the other illnesses!

Miss Reber who was in the adjacent room was sound asleep. And to this day Miss Reber recounts this story with much laughter.

And now as my mind wandered back to Mrs. Lee talking, I could see her worried face as she persevered, "And girls, pads are not to be used for playing."

"Playing?" I thought, "Who would want to play with that?"

Mrs. Lee added she knew a mother who had a little girl who was playing doctor and she used the pad to cover her face. Her mother was so mortified because they had guests visiting.

We quickly finished darning and thanked Mrs. Lee. We dashed downstairs and saw that the game had ended.

Some older girls came over and asked, "What took so long?

Lots of holes?

We laughed, "No, Mrs. Lee told us about growing up and how we're going to bleed."

"What?" the alarmed Cottage girls asked. "Bleeding once a month," we clamored.

"Oh, she told you about your period," they

215

commented. "Not period, bleeding," we corrected.

"No, it's period," stated Boots, "but we call it monthly."

"That's what it's called?"

"Yeah."

"But she didn't tell us that," we answered.

"I don't think Mrs. Lee knows those words," another girl replied. "In our Hygiene class at school they call it menstruation, but it's just easier to say monthly or period."

"You girls are lucky she told you about it."

"Did you know when Isabel took off her raincoat there was blood all over?"

"There was?"

"She didn't even know what happened. She didn't know about period."

Isabel was such a timid girl. "Poor Isabel," we gasped. Then I remembered Isabel's expression. Her eyes were so soulful like a cocker spaniel's and she had looked so bewildered as girls asked her what happened. They thought she was hurt, but then no more was said. Isabel was not hurt, she was mysteriously all right!

"But what's worse is what happened to Rhoda."

"Worse?" we asked alarmed.

"Yeah, worse than Isabel. No one knew Rhoda was bleeding, so every time she saw blood on her underpants she thought she was dying. She was so scared, she even threw her pants away."

"Oh no!" we cried in stunned horror. "That's scary, poor Rhoda."

"Yeah, so I guess that's why Mrs. Lee had to tell you."

"Wow!" we murmured.

That evening as I used the toilet, I checked my underpants, no blood yet. Days later I was still checking, nothing. Soon I forgot.

Then one day, Carol and I asked permission to go to a neighbor's house across the road at the back entrance to the Home. There were young twin blonde boys in the family whom we played with for years. Since they had not come over that day, we yelled loudly, "Henry and Herbie can you come over to play?" They didn't answer. We asked Miss Hayes' permission to go to their house; she reluctantly let us go. "Yea!" we cried. We felt adventuresome as we crossed the middle of the road for we were actually going to a friend's house. We ran up their gravel driveway and knocked on their front door. We waited on their tiny front porch.

Nursery group at Santa Cruz with Henry and Herbie (on left). Mrs Petterson & baby Donnie (on right)

Henry and Herbie were fun to play with because they were refreshing and different. Throughout the years they were the only boys we played with but they played the same things we did, although it was more fun because now they could be the fathers!

Their oldest sister Norma opened the door, eyed us and in a slothful voice while chewing on gum spat out, "Yeah?"

"Can Henry and Herbie come over to play?"

"I guess so," she turned her head, which was covered with strange looking bobby pin curls, and hollered at the top of her lungs, "Henry and Herbie, the girls want you to go over there to play!"

I was so surprised she yelled in the house. In the same monotone voice she mumbled, "Come in." She left us standing in the living room and we heard her yell again, "Henry and Herbie, the girls are here and they..." her voice trailed off. As we waited, I glanced around the dingy house, it was cluttered. My eyes fell on an empty waste basket with a peculiar looking object at the bottom. It was stiff and curved up at both ends. "Ugh!" I looked again, it was an old, used, dried up Kotex pad! Now I knew why Mrs. Lee told us to wrap it in newspaper! I nudged Carol and whispered... but before I could finish telling her about the pad, Henry and Herbie emerged. They looked at us and they were uneasy and withdrawn, probably because their place was messy.

"Hi," we said, "Want to go play?" They nodded and finally smiled. I felt better. That was more like the Henry and Herbie we knew. We scampered down the stairs. I was glad to leave their house!

A few months later, while sitting on the toilet, I noticed some redness on my underpants. Looking closer I could see it was blood. I was having my first period!

I knocked on Mrs. Lee's bedroom door which was ajar.

"Mrs. Lee," I said urgently, "May I please have a belt and a pad."

A surprised Mrs. Lee gently smiled and asked, "Now Nona, you remember how to put it on?"

I nodded and thanked her.

Walking down the Lok Hin stairs the unfamiliar bulkiness felt awkward, in fact, this part of growing up seemed weird because everything about me still seemed the same.

Growing up also meant that soon I'd be old enough to get a perm like the Cottage girls. Any Cottage girl who wanted a perm had to save $5 for the cost and this privilege. It took many months to reach this goal and when it was reached Miss Hayes had to approve their request.

Only one girl at a time was granted permission for a Saturday appointment. And when that long awaited day arrived she was able to skip the usual afternoon nap and walked downtown to the beauty shop for her big day. This procedure took several hours and as the apprehensive girl endured the strong smelling solution applied to her hair, she would wonder if she had taken the right step. But generally, the girls -though terribly self conscious with all the stares and exclamations from us younger girls- were pleased with their new appearance.

And now as I looked around the yard for Carol, I couldn't find her. "Carol," I yelled. Then I saw Carol chugging up the driveway on Edna's bike. "Guess what Carol?"

"What?" she cried.

"I got my period."

Carol braked the bike, jumped off and exclaimed, "You did?"

"Uh-huh," I nodded.

"What's it like?"

"Nothing really, it's just there." "Does it hurt?"

"No, but I can feel a little trickle coming down and it feels warm."

"It does?"

"Yeah, and it feels funny when I walk." Carol looked me over. "It doesn't show." "That's good!" I answered.

"You know what, Carol?" "What?"

"Henry and Herbie are lucky they don't have to bother with any of this stuff."

Carol nodded.

"And you know what else, Carol?" "No, what?"

"Now I have to spend my allowance on Kotex!"

Carol thought for a second and replied, "Yeah, but I wish I could have my period too."

"What for?"

"So I can grow up also."

I looked at Carol's serious face and sympathized, "I

know what you mean."

According to Ruby Chow, who had lived at the Ming Quong Home next to Mills College, the black limousine was owned by the benefactor, Joe Shoong. He was the owner of the world-wide National Dollar Stores which opened the same time as the J.C. Penney's stores.

Joe Shoong had a niece, Velma Soo Hoo, who lived at Ming Quong (Mills) and on the third

Sunday of each month he had a driver deliver chicken to the Home.

As Ruby recalled, "In those days chicken was expensive. Every time the driver came, the girls would all peer out the windows because orphans rarely had any visitors."

And the tall Chinese man, (in the black shiny car) who delivered the "mystery boxes" to the Los Gatos home was Bill Kee.

Towering Bill married the shortest and tiniest Ming Quong girl, Helen. (way before my time!)

Today Helen has the distinction of being the "oldest" Ming Quong gal (around 90 years old in 1996!).

What a dynamo lady with the energy of a 30 year old!

Helen still resembles a beautiful porcelain "China doll," which was her nickname.

Like Helen said, "I was the last one born in my family and they didn't have enough to make me, that's why I'm so small!"

Chapter 23

War is Over

anguish cries the night...
thousands died for peace on earth
silent souls move on...

I laid in bed, my heart pounding. I had awaken from a terrifying nightmare. In the dream total darkness had surrounded me and I was perched on a steep cliff about to fall. This recurring dream always petrified me. But one time it had been worse and a teacher had to rouse me because I had been crying out for help. I hated these nightmares and was always relieved to find myself in my own bed. I would look around the dark room and make out familiar images of the girls beds and the high windows which brought me back to the present. What a relief. It always seemed so real. How could it not be real?

Wide awake, I'd ponder my dream. Why did I dream this scary scene over and over again? I was almost afraid to fall asleep again.

Back then we did not have the knowledge or even thought of analyzing our dreams. We thought they just happened for no apparent reason.

Since then I've learned that the subconscious mind at night reenacts your life; telling you about yourself. Or as a dream expert Betty Bethards believes, every part of your dream represents an aspect of yourself.

My dream could have meant I was blinded by emotion and couldn't find a way out of my trouble and that my life was out of control which may have been in the field of my temper or morals. Even as far back as the biblical days, the kings knew how important their dreams were so upon awakening each morning they summoned their wise men (astrologers) to interpret their dreams.

Now with my knowledge of dreams and remembering how I felt back then as a Starlight, my nightmares stemmed from my abandonment, coupled with the teacher's strict control over my life and my growing curiosity of ones body's development. Which in that puritanical era no one spoke about, which in turn led to feelings of guilt.

But on the surface my nightmare could also have been caused by the simple fact of being afraid of the dark. I never mentioned this fear to anyone, because I didn't want to be teased.

This fear became more bothersome when I was around 12 years of age, when it was my turn to be Miss Reber's assistant in preparing breakfast. This meant I had to be awakened by an alarm clock which was set and placed by my bed each night by my teacher. After awakening, I had to dress in the dark as everyone was still sound asleep. Then armed with a flashlight, I'd fearfully step out the door, tiptoe down the flight of stairs leading to the old barn, dash outside and rush across the front yard to get to the kitchen's back door. From the Lok Hin building to the main house seemed like an eternity, especially on blustery wintry mornings when I thought all that existed in the moment was my fright and my pounding heart. In my mind I did not know what creepy creatures, like a ghost, a dog or a wild animal lurked behind the water tower, the pepper tree or alongside the main house peering at me or ready to spring out at me! But if the unknown was a man that would be the worst thing because of what had happened at the Home.

This frightening episode remained fixed in my mind and whenever I thought of it I shuddered. It happened early one morning just before breakfast, when a startled teacher found a disheveled man sound asleep on the back porch adjacent to the Chinese classroom. Fortunately this screened porch which housed 2-3 beds was not occupied.

This sleeping area was only used when conditions became crowded. It was not a favorite place to sleep as any roomers were in full view of anyone walking by from the classroom and of course from the screen door of the back porch. (But yet it was a step up between being a Lok Hin girl and a Cottage girl.)

That night the intruder had been a sailor stationed at Moffett Field. And when the younger girls had overheard the older girls using the word, "sailor" they were startled and asked, "Was it Earnest?" An annoyed girl replied, "Of course not, Earnest wouldn't do that."

"Who was it then?" they questioned.

And she replied, "He was a drunk sailor!"

And because the older girls knew we wouldn't understand, they said no more.

So in our minds, whatever drunk meant sounded really bad, for the man had also been abusive and threatening to the teacher and she in turn had to call the police.

After that incident a hook & eye was attached to the screen door, but to me that locking device seemed to flimsy. I dreaded the day I would grow up and have to sleep on that porch. But the inevitable happened when I was around 13 years old and had to move to that porch.

I was terrified each night. I would look at that screen door expecting to see a man's silhouette. I would just lay there for what seemed like hours and if I heard a strange sound, I'd stiffen. In the morning when the bell awakened me, I was exhausted!

At that time the Home hired a night watchman to check our grounds once during the night. Miss Hayes placed a time-clock in the old open garage which the watchman used indicating the time he had arrived to perform his job. Miss Hayes had told us never to touch this important clock. We never did.

And now with these hidden fears inside me I'd race into the kitchen, my heart still pounding, and I would then greet Miss Reber. "Good morning, Miss Reber."

"Good morning, Nona."

I never thought to tell Miss Reber about my fears for after all, they were only my own imaginings. And I didn't really want to take the chance that she might think I was childish!

Once inside, the warm familiar kitchen eased my mind. I loved the way the kitchen glowed at that time of the morning when all else was dark outside. I felt so safe and secure, like a baby enveloped in its mother's womb.

Soon all my fears were forgotten as I helped Miss Reber dish out the separate bowls of fruit for each person. Together we buttered slices of white bread with white oleo which had been mixed with orange colored granules to make the oleo look like real butter. I thought it would be really nice when we could have real butter again, but because of the war's ration stamps, Miss Reber had to be extra careful with the grocery money. We lined up trays of these buttered bread and placed them in the hot oven to be baked. Even though the oleo tasted bad, when baked in this manner, the crispy toast was one of my favorite parts of breakfast. Next I checked the sugar bowls and filled them if necessary and then poured five pitchers full of milk for the mush, all the while keeping a watchful eye and stirring the hot chocolate milk on the burner to keep it from scorching or worst boiling all over the stove. Meanwhile for our constitution, Miss Reber had a huge tea kettle of hot water boiling. And the steam as usual fogged up the small kitchen windows, shutting out the outside world.

After everything was in order, it was time to race upstairs to the small annex next to the infirmary and the classroom where a brass bell was kept on its own separate table. No one was permitted to touch that big bell, except the assigned girl on duty. With both hands held tightly I rang the first morning bell with all my might. This was a very important job for it was my responsibility to awaken the entire household, because if anyone overslept and was late for breakfast, the blame might be placed on me! But usually no one was late, as the ringing of the bell could even be heard by our neighbors! The poor neighbors could tell time by our bells! As I rang the bell, daylight was breaking and I was glad to see the light.

Once again my thoughts shifted to my fears. I thought of the weekly radio programs, The Inner Sanctum which, now as Lok Hin girls we were allowed this listening privilege. This horror program which we all loved probably compounded my phobia though I cannot recall what the stories were about. This horror program came on a half hour before bedtime. The evening of the program found us rushing through our toilet rituals, jumping into our pajamas and once huddled in bed and the lights off, we were ready. We'd listened intently to the storyteller's crackly voice as he bellowed his infamous laugh and chillingly closed the program with the eerie sounds of a squeaky closing door. He would always conclude by rasping, "I'll be back!" That left us screaming as we ducked our heads under the covers to stifle our outburst. Goosebumps covered my entire body as I scooted all the way down inside my bed!

But by far the most terrifying fear which occurred during the war years was to be awakened by air-raid sirens screaming in the night, paralyzing our bodies. Trembling, we immediately grabbed our bathrobe at the foot of our bed, stepped into our slippers and followed our teacher down the unlit stairway with her flashlight barely lighting the way through the pitch black main house to the playroom. Because the playroom was almost entirely below street level, it was used as our bomb shelter. Stacked alongside one of the walls was a huge stack of mattresses ready to be laid out if necessary for these emergencies. Special black shades were pulled down from the small high windows to block out any lights.

Nights like this were known as "black-outs," which

meant lights could not be turned on, because if the enemy planes saw them, they would bomb us! It seemed we experienced more black-outs in Los Gatos because we were close to Moffett Field. Scared and shaking we huddled together for comfort and warmth. Some of the younger girls whimpered. The teachers and some of the older girls quickly soothed them, telling them it was just a drill and it would be over soon and everything would be okay. Miss Chew would sometimes read a story, with the aid of a small stubby candle, and the little ones would be momentarily lost in the story. By the light of the flickering candle our shadowy

figures appeared ominous and that alone was scary enough!

One night we waited longer than usual, about 45 minutes or so, for the "all clear siren" to sound, indicating that all was well and we could go back to bed. But nothing happened. Edna got impatient and hoisted herself up on the narrow shelf above the cubby holes and balanced herself on one elbow. She lifted one corner of the shade and peered out. Someone hissed, "Get down, the enemy might see us and bomb us!"

"What did you see?" the girls whispered.

"Nothing, I couldn't even see the lights of San Jose!"

Hearing this, some Nursery girls began to cry and that's when the teachers decided to lay out the mattresses, with the help of the older girls. Cold and miserable, some managed to fall asleep.

All during these scary nights we felt a little sense of security as our silver war tags worn around our necks day and night identified us by name. We thought if the enemy saw or read our ID tags they would know we were from the Home and not separate us.

During one of these air-raids (when I was around 9 years of age) I became separated from everyone! I was just suddenly not in the room! I had vanished! When someone realized I was gone, my teacher, Miss

Davies, went looking for me. She found me upstairs sound asleep in my own bed!

This happened once again when I was in the Lok-Hin group. Both these times, I never recalled leaving the

Girls with ID tags. From left – Edna Mae, Xenia, Paula, Carol, Ida, Nora, Beverly, Nona

playroom. It seemed sleep-walking and fear of the dark had nothing in common! As an adult, I learned that sleep-walking was brought on by stress. My stress? The air-raid sirens!

As was the Home's routine, our prayer groups met every night after dinner. At that time I was in Mrs. Lee's group. One particular night we gathered in her bedroom and sat on our chairs in a circle with our heads bowed. Because of the war we always knew Mrs. Lee would be praying for the war to end. But tonight was different as she also prayed for Howard and his family, for as she continued, Howard had died in the war. I was puzzled, who was Howard?

227

1st row left Paula. Ida far right. 2nd row Nona, Carol, Beverly, Nora. 3rd row Alice, Edna, Mary Jane.

There was a strained silence in the room, followed by a muffled sob from the direction of Nora's chair. It was then I realized Howard was Nora's oldest brother.

I was numb. Someone we knew had actually died in the war! We did not know Howard personally, but we knew about him and what he looked like, because Nora's oldest sister Pansy kept a framed picture of Howard dressed in his army uniform on the Cottage dresser the girls shared. Many times we would ask Pansy if we could see her brother's picture. When she agreed, we always felt privileged to enter the Cottage domain! Pansy was very proud of her brother and that picture. But that portrait always left me with an uncomfortable feeling as his face was extremely rigid, his eyes seemed transfixed and his army cap seemed too small for his head.

2nd row, left
Frances Gok,
Jenny. 4th
row, Gloria,
Far right,
Isabel

I never knew if anyone else saw Howard that way, but I kept my thoughts to myself. They were not important. What I liked was Pansy's sharing and that she was proud of her brother.

And now as Nora's muffled sobs became louder, some sniffles came from the rest of us. Mrs. Lee ended the prayer. When our heads were lifted, everyone was crying. As we got up to leave, we clustered around a sobbing Nora. Some girls reached out and placed their hands on her shoulder. Our hankies were soaked and our bodies limp from the sadness.

That night in bed I couldn't sleep, my thoughts were about Nora and the war. War was so mean...why did her brother have to die and why did the family have to suffer so much?

That night, after my own personal prayer was said for Nora and her family, I drifted off into a fitful sleep, mindful that an air- raid siren might awaken us and everything would start all over again.

Sometime later the radio was turned on louder than usual and it filled the reception room with joyous sounds. While the younger girls were outside playing, a small group of Lok Hin and Cottage girls along with a few teachers gathered around as we heard President Roosevelt's voice declaring peace. Amidst shouts, cheers and loud horns the President's voice came through the radio clearly and exuberantly. We heard his voice proudly proclaiming, "THE WAR IS OVER!" We jumped and cheered quietly as we remembered we were in the house. Our excitement mounted as Miss Hayes told us to go outside and celebrate. And for this occasion Miss Hayes even let us use the front door! We felt like guests in our own home! We rushed out to the front porch where the rays of the sun shone down on us like pure gold. The graceful acacia trees blowing gently in the breeze fanned our jubilant faces. It seemed as if the sun and the trees joined forces with us in our celebration. Like Russian children around their Maypole, we joined hands and laughed as we pranced around the lone almond tree. We shouted at the top of our lungs, "THE WAR IS OVER! THE WAR IS OVER!"

Hearing our exalted voices, the Nursery girls came scampering up from the playground to join in the celebration. We clasped hands with them and we all chorused. "The war is over," and their little faces exploded with gales of laughter.

Prancing around the almond tree again and again reminded me of Edna's popular blue and white bicycle. With her bike we always rode circles around this tree. It was the only bike at the Home and Edna shared it with everyone who asked her. We'd ask, "Edna can we ride your bike?"

"Okay," she answered, "soon as I'm through," and we'd watch her expertly round the tree and sail down the long driveway, passed the playground, and zoom back up to the front yard and circle the tree once more. She paused and almost got off, but changed her mind and once again repeated the process which made us impatient. We couldn't wait for our turn to ride like Edna.

We lined up and took turns round and around the almond tree, teetering, screaming as we learned. The poor bike was banged so many times as we'd fall and crash it unmercifully. About twice a month there'd be a flat tire and patient Edna with a friend would ask permission to walk to the gas station to pump up the tire. Poor Edna, we tried to help her and volunteered to walk it down but Miss Hayes said, "It's Edna's bicycle and she's responsible."

In "regular families", if it was not war time, the bike would probably have been driven to the gas station, but it never even entered our minds that Miss Reber could have driven it to the station, for that was not her job or her responsibility. Besides, gas was rationed also.

We'd wait anxiously for their return as the station was a mile away and when we spotted them, I could see Edna's flushed face and they'd be drenched with sweat from pushing the bike uphill. "They're back, they're back!" we clamored. "Thanks Edna!"

we yelled and eagerly we'd start all over again, grateful that the tire was once again able to be patched. For if it couldn't be fixed, that would mean the bike would be useless, because the gas station attendant had told Edna, there were no more bicycle tires to be bought because all available rubber now had to be saved and used for the war.

Once again we were lucky, but that didn't last long because the tires soon wore out completely.

And now, looking around the yard I saw that some of the teachers were actually outside enjoying our enthusiasm and for a change they looked really happy and carefree. But among the jumping girls I glimpsed Pansy's face and felt sad but noticed she too was celebrating along with her sisters. I was glad.

I left the celebration to go to the closet bathroom which was adjacent to the kitchen. Leaving the bathroom, I heard boisterous noises coming from the kitchen. Peering in I saw the Cottage girl, Bernice, who was on kitchen duty. I could see her smiling profile. I never failed to notice her glasses which were so thick they made her eyes appear as two little beads lost in orbit! She was laughing hysterically and shouting, "Yeah, we won the war against the Japs!"

The word "Jap" stunned me. I couldn't believe what I just heard! I peered in again and I could see Miss Reber smiling at Bernice's enthusiasm. Holding my breath, I watched Miss Reber's face but her expression did not change. It was as if she had not heard Bernice's forbidden word. That was just like Miss Reber! She was so kind-hearted, she could not spoil Bernice's happiness. No one was around as I quietly left the playroom and went outside to join the cheerful girls. I wondered why Bernice had not learned what Miss Hayes had taught us years ago. Could there be that much hate and resentment against the Japanese people? Because she was older did she know other things I don't know?

By now my joy had diminished as I felt a gnawing hurt inside me. It pained me to hear the word "Jap". I realized I had learned the lesson of discrimination well from Miss Hayes. I looked at Miss Hayes' smiling face; she looked really pleasant. At that moment, deep inside me, I felt what it was like to be a true Christian. And I was grateful that many years ago Miss Hayes had been strict with us and had taught us to respect others.

After the day's joyous celebration, I crawled into bed that night emotionally spent, yet content. I prayed, thanking God that the war had ended.

Now life would be back to normal for us and the whole country. No more men killed or maimed for life and no more heart-broken families. Miss Reber could now shop without counting those tiny ration stamps. We could now take off our bothersome ID tags and use the chain for playing hopscotch! And now, maybe even Edna's mother could buy her new bicycle tires! Tonight the countryside was quiet and serene. As usual the stars were sparkling and even milky-way looked clear! I knew nothing could mar this tranquility, for finally after five years we could fall asleep in peace.

Chapter 24

Moving On

passages of time
ever changing - renewing
chapters completed

At 13, I had chopstick legs and was one of the tallest and skinniest girls at the Home.

I looked in the full-length, three-way mirror with the store's bright light reflecting my shapeless form and Beverly's remarks of how she perceived me came to mind, "Straight up and down, with no sides!" That was definitely true. It was obvious menstruation was not making my figure bloom!

Beverly's dry wit had made me laugh. But funny or not, that was how we were at the Home. We thought from our hearts and our answers were straightforward and quick, with no thought of malice. Ask a Ming Quong girl her opinion and she would always tell you the truth.

As we grew older, if any remarks did bother us, we took care of it ourselves, with no assistance from a teacher. Sometimes we'd argue or we'd laugh and sometimes we'd pretend it made no difference. But in general, we learned that the best way to get over a "hurt" was to confide in a friend. We also knew that what was said was the truth and the sooner we accepted that fact, the better off we would be; therefore the ambiance at the Home was mostly peaceful.

The teachers had set good examples and never disagreed in front of us. If there was any strife amongst themselves, presumably they took care of it during their daily morning sessions when we were away at school.

Now as I continued to gaze at the store's mirror my

eyes wandered beyond myself. I could see the Lok Hin girls and a few Cottage girls checking out the many racks of dresses. A feeling of happiness embraced me for today was the highlight of our vacation from school, and was also the fruit of our summer's work. Today was our annual shopping for school clothes at the Hart's department store in San Jose. It was exciting to be in San Jose at this large store, for compared to the small stores in Los Gatos, this store appeared to take up the whole city block. The other stores in Los Gatos did not offer the selections of dresses we needed in our price range. But we did buy our Buster Brown shoes at the family-owned Crider's shoe store in town.

This year Miss Hayes brought along Miss Bergman to help her. Miss Bergman was a kind soul, who once, after I remarked about her well-groomed nails, had taken the time to manicure mine.

One summer day she told me to come to see her after my nap. I had knocked on her bedroom door (adjacent to Mrs. Lee's). No answer. I knocked again.

I heard nothing and was about to try again when I heard a muffled voice.

"Who is it?"

"It's Nona, Miss Bergman." "What is it, Nona?"

"You told me to come after my nap and you would show me how to take care of my nails."

Silence.

The door opened and I was not prepared for what I saw. Miss Bergman was not her usual self. Strands of silver hair hung in front of her face, her dress was crumpled and she was disoriented. I was taken back.

"Oh, excuse me," she apologized. "I was taking a nap."

I was speechless. Taking a nap! I thought that was weird. Here we hated to take naps and now Miss Bergman took one, even when she didn't have to.

I then apologized for waking her. Disappointed I

turned to leave.

"No, no, I promised," she insisted, ushering me in.

For my lesson she laid a clean white hand towel on top of a small table, placing a small container and assorted miniatures implements on top.

"All this?" I asked.

She nodded. To me, it resembled a dentist table! But I knew I was in for a treat.

She soaked my fingertips in the small container in a special solution, pushed down the softened cuticles with an implement, cleaned under my nails, buffed my nails with a funny-looking buffer and then applied a clear coat of polish. I was amazed. I never knew I had so many half moons! She finished off with a dab of hand lotion.

Miss Bergman was so patient.. I never realized how long it took her to be well groomed. No wonder she was tired! All during my session she yawned and yawned.

I thanked her profusely. She smiled and replied, "You're welcome" and closed the door. I think she went back to bed.

That day, I proudly showed my beautiful nails to some girls.

They questioned, "Miss Bergman did it?" "Yes."

"Really?"

"Yeah, you can go there too."

And off they went. I don't know how long Miss Bergman continued this procedure, but she was one fine teacher with a grand persona and a stylish appearance. And for our sake we were glad Miss Hayes needed her assistance.

Now at the store I pivoted in front of the mirror and asked Rhoda, "What do you think of this dress?" Before she could reply Miss Hayes walked by and said tersely, "You've got nothing on top, let Harlan try it on."

Mortified I left for the dressing room. "Here," I said to Harlan as I handed her the dress. "Miss Hayes wants you to try this on." As Harlan emerged from the dressing room and surveyed herself in the mirror, Miss Hayes approvingly said to Miss Bergman, "She's got all the bumps and curves." Miss Bergman did not acknowledge her. Harlan's faint smile conveyed her embarrassment, but I knew she felt pleased with Miss Hayes' comment.

Miss Hayes' quip made me self conscious. I glanced at Miss Hayes as she surveyed Harlan's figure and reveled in her own pleasure.

Miss Hayes' delight reminded me of the time when I was about 7 years of age and was a Starlight. We had been napping when we saw our teacher very purposefully tip-toeing and peeking in through the French doors to spy on us! Fortunately for us we were resting and not talking.

Shortly after the teacher left the fire alarm went off. We stiffened because the jarring sound, though not as alarming as an air-raid siren, always scared us. But we knew it was not a real fire, because we never ever had a fire at the Home. But nevertheless the drills were inevitable.

Whenever we heard the alarm go off we had to quickly put on our bathrobes and head toward the emergency exit. Each group had their own set of emergency stairs.

But that day was not to be the usual routine drill because of our carelessness. As we lunged for our bathrobes at the foot of our bed, they were not there! Uh-oh! We had broken the rules by not putting our bathrobes at the end of the bed. We rushed towards the large dressing room closet and to our surprise we saw Miss Davies blocking the way.

"Excuse us, Miss Davies," we cried, "We have to get our bathrobes."

But instead of moving out of the way, Miss Davies flung both arms out like an eagle in flight and stated, "You know the rules. It's a fire drill, go outside immediately."

"But, but..."

"Go," she repeated firmly.

We could not believe this was happening. We looked at Miss Davies' determined expression as she continued to maintain her stance. We were stunned; for with all the other fire drills we had always been able to grab our robes and rush outdoors. But now Miss Davies was acting like a mechanical robot carrying out a particular order. We were completely humiliated, for we had nothing on but our underpants. We crossed our arms over our chests as we walked across the front yard to our designated places. All the other startled girls stared at us and from the corner of my eye, I could see our gardener snickering.

Miss Hayes' mouth spread out into a triumphant grin and she looked at our crossed arms and gloated, "What if it had been a real fire and the fireman had come, what would you have done?" We said, "nothing," but inside I thought she was the meanest teacher at the Home.

We were at fault, but we couldn't get over the fact that Miss Hayes enjoyed our predicament. That day we learned our lesson well!

And now as I continued to search through the racks of dresses, Rhoda whispered to me, "Nona, you shouldn't feel so bad. Did you know Mrs. Lee gave me a brassiere to wear?"

"Huh?" I said, astonished.

"Yeah, I was so embarrassed because I didn't even know how to wear it and I'm the only one she gave it to."

I looked at Rhoda's blushing face and felt the painful paradox, everyone had their problems.

Rhoda went on, "You know what I do when I have to hang my clothes out to dry?"

"No, what?" I asked.

"I hide the brassiere in my clothes pin bag. That way no one can see it while it dries on the line."

"You do?" I gasped.

She nodded "Yes," and we laughed softly. Poor Rhoda, first bleeding and now hiding her brassiere!

I had never noticed Rhoda's figure, probably because

she was overweight, but I couldn't imagine what it would be like to have Rhoda's problem and have to hide a brassiere. I guess her period worked quickly.

Looking back I think a teacher should have shown Rhoda the fundamentals of putting on a brassiere. But to the teachers raising us, each day was a new learning experience and Rhoda was just ahead of the teachers. In fact, Rhoda was left down in Los Gatos a long time after her age group had left (till age 15) for the Oakland Home. No explanation was given to her then, but she found out (as an adult) she was needed to help assist Miss Reber. As Rhoda put it, "It seemed I was in the kitchen all my life."

Now trying to find just the right dress for school reminded me of the time I had been given the most beautiful dress in the world for free. What a day that was. But I knew in this store I would not find a dress like that, because that dress had been a one-of-a-kind dress.

That day the Home had received a huge box of excess dresses from a clothing store. That unexpected gesture surprised and thrilled us.

Many excited "Oohs" escaped from us as the teachers pulled out one pretty dress after another and handed them out to the girl whom they thought it would fit. We all hoped with all our hearts that at least one dress would fit.

The one that did fit me well was made of the softest fabric I'd ever seen or felt. The color was deep red, almost burgundy, and trimmed in a luxurious navy velvet. I wore this dress to church almost every Sunday, till I outgrew it and finally had to pass it on to Bernice Wong, who had admired it.

That day after everyone had tried on the dress, there were still some left that didn't fit anyone. Rhoda was one of them, because of her large size.

Poor Rhoda, she told me at age 15, she weighed 140 pounds. I don't know if she ever heard what the girls use to chant, "Fatty, fatty, two by four, can't get through the kitchen door." (This rhyme was just fun to say and hear

239

and we would chant it repeatedly. It was never really directed to anyone in particular and we didn't even really know what we were saying.)

As an adult, Rhoda told me that she used to refer to herself as the "baby Kate Smith," (a popular overweight singer in the 1930s). "At the Home I was depressed, because of my weight and looks. Now when I look back at my Ming Quong pictures, I looked like an old lady and my hair had no style. But then, all of a sudden I woke up and realized life is worth living."

After leaving the Home, Rhoda, Emma and I were roommates in Oakland. And like the Home, we alternated our household duties. When it came to cooking dinner, all Rhoda wanted was vegetables. I used to watch her enjoy a half a head of raw cabbage for dinner and she ate it like it was the best gourmet treat around.

Today, people are amazed that she was once overweight. She is now one of Ming Quong's most glamorous girls!

And back to that "free dress day." After everyone was done, Miss Hayes looked over at the extra dresses and not wanting to see these dresses go to waste, she decided to bundle up the remainder and send them to an exclusive private school in the vicinity.

We all had thought that was a great idea. But back came the box of dresses along with a haughty note, "We do not accept charity!"

We were astounded and Miss Hayes along with the teachers were flabbergasted. Miss Hayes had unknowingly insulted the administrator. Miss Hayes had learned a lesson, which reminded me about Maria and her mother. I could now understand why Miss Hayes had been apprehensive when I had pleaded with her for the dress for little Maria. But did she know how Maria's mother might react? I don't think so. Miss Hayes did it from the kindness of her heart and also so I'd stop asking! As for me, I knew what I learned from this exchange, if you're poor like Maria's parents or if you're well off like the private school, they all had one thing in common, monstrous egos, no manners, and no sense of appreciation.

My thoughts were interrupted by Miss Hayes' call, "Come on girls, finish shopping. It's almost time for lunch."

We scrambled and showed Miss Hayes the clothing we wanted. She and Miss Bergman checked and approved our apparel according to how they looked on us and to make sure we had kept within our particular budget. If we were over our allotted amount, we had to decide on which dress was best and that's when Miss Bergman's help was appreciated.

After shopping we crossed the street to our favorite hamburger diner. It was a small place with just a counter with one table in the back. But to us, it was the best restaurant in town because that was the only one we'd ever been in. We placed our usual orders for hamburgers, while some Cottage girls also ordered French fries and milkshakes. We were ecstatic, for we never had a piece of meat this size and grilled this way at the Home. This restaurant was always jammed with a hungry lunch time crowd and there was never any room for us, so we headed towards the St. James park and sat on the picnic benches. Taking a bite of my juicy hamburger, I looked up at the tall pine trees and felt the soft wind brush against my face. I smiled; life was wonderful.

But my joy was short-lived for unbeknownst to me my days at the Home were numbered!

And that day came when Miss Hayes called us to her office and told us we were of age to move to the other Ming Quong Home in Oakland, near Lake Merritt. The other girls were pleased, but I was devastated. I listened but didn't hear as my childhood flashed through my head. I didn't want to leave this home I had grown to love.

I quickly left the office and walked outside to the front

241

yard. I stumbled around in a daze and tears streamed down my face as I hurriedly brushed them away.

A familiar voice startled me. "Nona, why are you crying?"

I turned around and saw a blurry figure made hazy by my tears and the sun's rays. It was Miss Bankes, the former head of the Home.

I wondered where she came from and why she was here. Was she visiting for the day?

Quaking, I replied, "Because I have to move."

Squinting, she said, "Nona, think of your life as a book. You are growing up and it's time to move on.

Circa 1943

You're closing one chapter and beginning another. That's what I did when I left here. I, too, ended a chapter."

Miss Bankes' words made sense and as I looked at her I felt a new flood of tears surfacing. It seemed Miss Bankes actually cared!

She handed me her handkerchief. I didn't want to use it, but she insisted. I thought of her comments and realized she had gone through this same experience, but I could not fathom her departure as painful for she had always seemed devoid of any feelings. She had never seemed real to me, for she never appeared like a person who would listen to your problems.

Then through my misty eyes I saw a faint smirk on her

face. She seemed to be enjoying my misery. Perturbed, but undaunted, I stood steadfast, ignoring her expression. I thought of how she viewed life, it seemed so simple; just close a chapter and move on!

I thought of my life and realized I had already gone through various chapters, but why, I thought, did each chapter have to be so painful?

Miss Higgins,
Miss Bankes

Amongst the amaryllis belladonnas

Two Nursery girls walked by and threw curious glances our way. I turned away. My tears had stopped and to my surprise I felt better. I realized my talk with Miss Bankes, though disturbing, had been beneficial. Returning her handkerchief, I thanked her and left.

The next morning I woke to the sounds of birds singing and realized the day I dreaded had arrived. My eyes fell on the small carton box on the floor. Packed inside was everything I owned. I dressed slowly and stepped outside. The morning was serene and beautiful, the clear sky was filled with patches of fluffy clouds. As I walked to the dining room for breakfast, the garden was bathed in dew and the early morning rays of the sun warmed my body.

I looked at the familiar pepper tree arching over the stone rock bench and in the raised flower bed a few amaryllis belladonnas beckoned to me. Bending over I inhaled deeply and as usual the lilting fragrance filled me with delight. At that moment I forgot my sadness.

I adored these stately lilies and loved their delicate shade of pink. Ending my euphoric mood with an appreciative "aah" I was reminded that even flowers go through cycles. From an odd- shaped bulb germinating in the dark ground to tiny spikes of leaves pushing forth in winter gradually covering the bed with a rich carpet of slender long leaves.

I wondered if the Home in Oakland had flowers. As I approached the main house I gazed around at my beloved surroundings; and something deep within me quickened my senses and I felt compelled to implant these beautiful images in my soul forever.

Main house, Annex & Infirmary

After breakfast we piled into the shiny black car with Miss Higgins, a stout, formidable figure who was a former teacher from "Nine-twenty" and the Ming Quong Home near Mills College. She was now the administrator for both the Los Gatos and Oakland homes.

As we drove down the driveway, the Nursery girls ran after the car yelling, "Good-bye, good-bye." But I could hardly respond for I felt this deep heaviness and my whole being knew that this was it, I was leaving. And in leaving, I was in essence leaving my mother behind.

Close to 12 years had passed since my mother first left me at the Home. I remembered how I thought she would come back for me and how I had planned to show her around the house before we left. Though the pain had subsided many years ago, this reality of moving on brought back the mourning process. But only in the sense of a deeper awareness. I wanted to thank my mother for her insight. For whatever the reason she left me here, I'm sure she knew back then that this Home would provide for me.

I held back my tears and silently thanked her.

As the car rounded the bend, I looked back for the last time and all the children and the teachers were still waving. I knew that today was also a sad day for the remaining girls, especially the young ones for they too would miss us. And I knew they would continue to wave till the car was out of sight. I waved back and in my heart I said my goodbyes, goodbye to everything I loved and knew.

Chapter 25

Questions, Questions

chopstick childhood
seeking answers...finding peace
radiant light shines...

Growing up, I've asked so many questions concerning my roots, I became as St. Augustine said, a question to myself. Hundreds of ordinary questions that most people take for granted is information I've hungered for. Where was I born? What was my mother and father like? How did they meet? What did they look like? Did I look like my mother or did I look like my father? Other cultural questions such as, was my mother from China?

Was their marriage arranged? Did my father go back to China for his bride? Who were my grandparents and great-grandparents?

Answers to some of these questions came mostly when I was in my teens. When I was living at the Oakland Home as a teenager, some teacher (I can't recall who) told me I was born in Menlo Park. I had never heard of Menlo Park, although I had an idea it must be on the Peninsula, because that was my county (Santa Clara County) where my family was from. Nevertheless, I was really happy to know my place of birth. And I liked the unique idea of being born in a park!

Right away, I came up with this game. I'd ask the girls, "Guess where I was born?"

"Where?" they chorused seriously (for they were aware that I never knew my place of birth.)

And I daringly replied, "In a park."

Their astonished voices cried out, "A park?" "Yeah, a real park."

246

Waiting for my explanation, I laughed, "Menlo Park!" Later, I learned the correct facts, that I was really born in Palo Alto. Darn, no more fun games!

Seriously, though, most of my other answers came from Ellen (and a few relatives) for as I became an adult, Ellen and I became quite close.

But starting at the beginning, I was told at Ming Quong that my relatives were from Northern China, because people from that region were tall and refined. It was instilled in me that these attributes were something to be proud of. And so I was proud, to a certain extent, but I saw nothing really wonderful about being gangly. And as for being refined, I guess I was because I was more reserved than the other Chinese girls at the Home. (Reflecting back, I don't think this had anything to do with the Chinese culture, of being reticent or reserved, because this was just my make-up.)

But in 1996, at our Mock family picnic at Riconando Park in Palo Alto, a gold-mine of information came my way. Although we had about 17 of these family gatherings, each family group generally kept within their own circle. When I did speak to my relatives, it was always just surface talk, "Hello, how are you?" This was especially directed to the older relatives, whom I thought were distant. This, I'm sure, stemmed back to the Los Gatos time at the Home when my relatives visited and I felt like I was not a part of their world and remembering their stiffness. I'm sure they felt uncomfortable also.

But at this picnic, I received facts that I'd never heard from Ellen, because my father's youngest brother Hank was there (after an absence of about 14 years). In fact, it was this outgoing uncle that started these Mock picnics.

As uncle Hank told me, one day he was in a store and he saw two Chinese girls and struck up a conversation with them. When he asked their names, he was completely flabbergasted, for they were his nieces! These girls were his brother's (Hong You) daughters!

As Hank related, "I thought we should have these picnics, for here we are walking around and we don't ever know our own relatives!"

He got together with Ellen and it became a family tradition. But at the second or third picnic, some misunderstanding arose between Hank and Ellen, so Hank and his family never returned. And now to see him again, was like the prodigal son returning to the fold.

I was happy, for uncle Hank, who is seven years older than me, was different from the other relatives. He was updated, gregarious and full of life. The timing was perfect, for now I could finalize my research.

But first I spoke to Awah (because I had encountered her first). Awah was the wife of the now deceased Hong You. She was born and raised in China, adjacent to the Mock village. I was elated because now I had firsthand information about my relatives in China. She said our family was from Southern China, Guanazhou, (formerly Canton) and that our village was in Southern China, not in the north as Mrs. Lee had told me.

Back at the Home, what Mrs. Lee told me, I believe, was her honest belief. For when my relatives visited me, she saw that they were tall and refined. And we were, especially Emma, whose aloofness and mannerisms equaled those of a high society debutante.

In China, people with the same surname lived in their own village. And as Awah related, the Mock villagers dressed in solid colored peasant shirts and pants. They lived simply in small houses made of concrete. Each house had an entrance with no door and the window in the house was the same. Kerosene and candles were used at night. Their water was from a common well, which was utilized by the entire village. Their toilet was a common pot used inside the house. And as Judy (Awah's daughter) related, raw sewage ran freely in the gutter outside the houses beside a narrow two-foot walkway next to each house.

Mosquitoes and flies swarmed constantly, and were even more a nuisance in the sticky tropical humid weather.

Hogs ran wild and chickens wandered in and out of the houses. A family pig was raised inside the house, not as a pet, but to be fattened and resold for another.

Though the Mock village seemed on the edge of poverty they did have an ox to till the soil for their vegetables, which was a luxury compared to some villages.

With the villagers living in those dire conditions, it was no wonder that the Ming Quong teachers talked about the starving people in China. Also the missionaries who sailed across the continent to offer their help and to bring the word of God to help lighten their plight in life, considered the Chinese to be heathens and definitely needed to be saved.

As history has shown in the mid 1800s, exciting tales of bountiful wealth spread from village to village about this far off land, Mai Gau (beautiful country) which advertised in the Chinese printed newspaper that, "The American people are the richest in the world. They welcome the Chinese. When you arrive in the United States, you will live in big houses, receive very high wages, have good food and nice clothes."

The villagers also listened to tales of gold in the mountains, just waiting to be discovered. These stories promised a wonderful life in America, away from China's oftentimes horrendous floods, droughts, famine and revolutions.

When the Mock villagers heard these stories, they too were eager to join the masses leaving China. And they were encouraged by their families to go seek their fortune and to come back for them.

As far as Ellen could figure out, grandpa and his first born son, (my father) left China in the early 1900s. But how they entered this country is a mystery, because of the

Chinese Exclusion Act of 1882 that Congress had passed forbidding any Chinese to enter the USA. The only ones allowed in were sons of US citizens or Chinese merchants. But most Chinese came in illegally.

And in my mind while gathering the above information, it came to me why Chinese people were more quiet and secretive, because of the simple fact that they were fearful of being caught and shipped back to China! Was this the next generation's new heritage of following their parent's footsteps of being reticent or reserved?

Oops, sorry, I'm completely digressing, but I think everything is interrelated.

Getting back to grandpa, according to Ellen, grandpa was probably in his mid twenties and my father about nine years of age, when grandpa left his young wife and daughter behind in China. Back then, Confucian belief dictated that a wife should stay to serve her husband's parents — but it was also harder to bring a family to a new country.

Grandpa bundled up his savings and took off with some villagers to gum-saun (gold mountain) as nicknamed by the villagers. If the villagers had no savings, they borrowed money on a credit system, and then repaid their debt after arrival in the new land. Another method involved signing a term contract of service for their passage. There were many abuses in these two systems, especially the contract method.

As far as Ellen knew, grandpa never used these methods as she never heard of grandpa owing money to anyone.

The villagers journeyed for close to three months shuttled in the confines of the ship's steerage. This crowded condition was worse than village living and many became ill and died.

When the ship arrived in America, the men debarked in San Francisco at the end of Montgomery Street, near the waterfront where a decrepit shack was used for their processing.

In this country, grandfather and my father migrated down to the peninsula and settled in the small unincorporated area of Palo Alto, known back then as Mayfield.

Grandfather leased acres of fertile fields, hired Chinese men and together they became vegetable growers. When the vegetables were ready to market, he had a driver truck his vegetables to the produce section in San Francisco.

Grandfather also utilized any extra plot of land to plant colorful asters and fragrant sweet-peas.

During this time grandfather regularly sent money back to China for his family.

After 20 years he had saved enough money and he made the long voyage back for his wife and daughter. (This daughter was the mother to Octavia and Ruby (my cousins) who lived at Ming Quong with me while their brothers Stephen, Bob (adopted), Ralph and Henry lived at Chung Mei.)

Meanwhile my father had his own business of selling vegetables and fruit door to door in his own semi-open truck equipped with a scale.

During this time my father married and Ellen was born. When Ellen was able, she joined the other women immigrant workers in the flower fields, plucking suckers from the plants. She also sold grandfather's flowers at the corner of Embarcadero Way and Louis Ave in Palo Alto.

But (as noted) after her mother passed away, Ellen became a domestic slave. Looking back at Ellen's horrific background, she at least had something simple that was a bright spot in her life. She could eat as many vegetables as she pleased, which made her very happy for she loved greenery and grandpa grew tons of wonderful vegetables.

One year his crop of celery was so huge he even had pictures taken that season. It was a fact that in the 1890s it was the Chinese who turned celery into a commercial crop (in Orange County). Because of the farming background in China, many Chinese possessed superior horticultural skills which benefited the development of American agriculture. The Bing cherry was named after Ah Bing. And a frost free orange was developed which won an award in 1911. Also during the early 20th century, new strains of rice were pioneered by the Chinese in California.

With grandpa's fine vegetables, Ellen was always strong and healthy.

Once in a while Ellen was able to visit us at the Home (with grandma). I remember one time she gave Emma and I sweaters. My maroon slip-on sweater had my initials in navy, crocheted on the front. I thought this was so clever. I ran my fingers across the raised initials and broke into a big smile. I loved this sweater and thought my sister who smiled down at me was so nice.

2nd row left – Nona with Ellen's sweater

The Sunday Miss Chew let me wear the sweater to church, I was so proud, especially when the curious girls asked, "Who's the sweater from?" Beaming, I replied, "It's from my big sister, she made it."

In our family, Ellen told me that all the babies born in our household were delivered at home by a Caucasian woman physician, Dr. Johnson. Because no one spoke English, she named all the babies. Now I finally knew why my name was unusual.

But my Chinese name was given to me by grandpa, who named all the children, as was the custom in our family. Ellen said that when I was born, which was on the 8th day of the month (the most coveted money-making number in China), the grandparents repeatedly said, "Yow gum, yow ngaun," meaning that I would have gold and silver. To me, this seemed so ironic, here my grandparents traveled halfway around the world for riches, and the closest they came to any semblance of wealth was from the birthdate of their youngest granddaughter! Although their life here was much better than village living.

Another unusual thing I learned about my Chinese name was at the Home, Mrs. Lee had taught me to write my Chinese name in different characters. Her particular characters actually meant, "the better things in life." This information came from a scholarly uncle (a cousin to Ellen's husband) raised in China and also reiterated by Awah.

When Mrs. Lee found out about this error, she simply stated that she had misunderstood. And I believed her, because Mrs. Lee only heard what was good for us!

And so unknowingly I went through life with two Chinese names. A name for my astrological sign Gemini, the twins? Anyway, I now like both my names!

At my birth, my parents had only two surviving children. The other two girls had died, the first one at 6 months (the cause was unknown to Ellen) and the second baby was stillborn. She said my mother cried for days over the loss of the stillborn and that her crying had made Ellen cry. Mother also grieved for the 6- month-old daughter, but her outward crying for the stillborn is still vivid in Ellen's mind. About three or four months after my birth, my father, who was in his early 40s, died of tuberculosis. Left with two young children and a baby (me!) during the depression years, my mother must have had a tremendous struggle most of the time. But according to my relatives my mother was not to be pitied for she was an independent woman. Her small home had two bedrooms and a half bath (no tub or shower) and was three blocks from the grandparents farm and their smaller run-down house. This close proximity was intolerable for my mother, with her temperament and her dislike for her overbearing mother-in-law.

Then one day, according to Ellen, when I was around 1 years old, the unexpected happened. That day Emma (who was around 6 years old) and John (one year younger) had walked over to the grandparent's house for the day. When they returned the house was strangely quiet. Mother and I were nowhere to be found. For mother and I had simply moved out! What a scary, shocking day for my poor siblings.

Emma and John were taken in by the grandparents. Mother never came back.

I remember once (when I was in my teens) Emma shared that our mother had a lot of beautiful jewelry and that once mother had let her try it on. This delighted Emma who especially loved her jade necklace. I asked Emma, "What happened to her jewelry?" She didn't know. To this day Emma covets Chinese jewelry, especially fine jade.

After my mother and I left, the grandparents and all their children moved into mother's house.

My mother and I had taken off from the vast quiet fields of Palo Alto to the steep, crowded hills of San Francisco's Chinatown teeming with the sounds and smells of Old China.

It was at this point where my story began.

During my stay at the Oakland Home when I was a teenager (approximately three years), Ellen also lived in Oakland, about four blocks from the Home. She was married and had a young son and a daughter. There would be family dinners at her home for Christmas and I would drop by once in a while on Saturdays to visit and sometimes stay for dinner. After dinner we would visit around the dining table. The subject occasionally came up about our background and my mother.

Ellen told me back then, when she lived in Palo Alto (probably in her late teens) that a person (I assume a Social Worker) had come to the house and questioned her about my mother. They only spoke to her, because no one else was home and grandma spoke only broken English. Ellen asked the person what was wrong with my mother. The reply was that she was sick and sent to a mental hospital. Sometimes Ellen talked about my mother being crazy (mentally) and how she was glad she didn't have that type of blood in her system, because she was safe, as were her children. I would listen in silence and wonder if she was implying I might go crazy too.

Sometime later, John, who was now living back in Palo Alto, became withdrawn and heard bells ringing in his head. Then when I was in high school in Palo Alto, John was seen walking on El Camino Real in the nude. He was picked up by the authorities and placed at the Napa State Hospital.

Poor John, I felt so sorry for him throughout his life. When the Chung Mei boys had visited us at the Home in Los Gatos, someone had told me he was my brother. I shyly walked up to him to say, "Hi," and I was in for a surprise. His face turned completely red and he turned away from me. I was stunned and wondered what was wrong, but I could see even then that he wasn't like the other Chung Mei boys. My brother was painfully shy and it hurt him to be confronted by me or anyone else.

So now Ellen had more fuel to back up about my mother's illness. I'm sure her children were glad their mother, Ellen, was not a blood relative of my mother.

After my marriage to Joe at age 19, we began a search for my mother. Mental hospitals had no record of her.

The fact that I was a Chinese orphan may have

complicated matters in finding my mother. For on my birth certificate my mother's name is Lum Shee, but it seemed many Chinese women's names were Lum Shee! This bizarre fact I learned from a friend (in my late 30s). I had told him proudly, "I finally know my mother's name." His reply was, "It doesn't make any difference, because my mother's name is the same!"

Three decades later, I learned that Chinese women from the old country retained their maiden name when they married and that's why there were so many Lum Shee names. Translated in English, Lum Shee means Miss Lum. At last, one more question answered!

Records of my stay at the Home are not around, for too many years have elapsed. I tried corresponding with the Donaldina Cameron house, and the present administrator, Reverend Harry Chuck, contacted Lorna Logan, the administrator before him. Lorna Logan took over after Donaldina Cameron and she remembered my name.

In 1994, I met a missionary assigned to the Donaldina Cameron House and I was given the rare opportunity to research their files. With the help of my husband and my friend, Jody, we searched and found nothing, except a group picture I had sent Miss Chew (as an adult) taken at a Ming Quong reunion. A year later, I searched through files in the attic of the Los Gatos Home with Tanya Lonac from Eastfield Ming Quong, but found no records.

And now back to the family picnic in 1996. After I talked to Awah, I took Hank aside and questioned him. He told me that my father was a gentleman and dressed nicely. He also said I looked like my mother and John looked like our father, for father like John had been a tall, slim, nice-looking man with a shock of black hair. As for Emma, she resembled both parents.

This answer seemed easy, but it was not, because when I was a teenager Ellen had told me the complete opposite, that it was I, not Emma who resembled both parents. At that time, I was disappointed because I wanted to look like my mother. But then, I thought it was nice to be a part of both my mother and father in appearance.

I told Ellen (at the picnic) what Hank had said and after giving it some thought, she then agreed.

At age 63, I finally had an accurate image of my mother. This feeling of truly knowing felt strange, yet it felt good at the same time. I sensed inside me a going back to an unknown history, like I had been moving forward where mother had stopped.

But as Jody pointed out, many people resemble one parent at one stage, another at another stage. In her situation, everybody referred to her as "her father's daughter" and now they tell her, she looks "just like her mother."

So from Jody, I learned this interesting concept.

Back at the picnic. I reminded Hank that my mother had taken me with her to San Francisco to live. That refreshed his memory, for at that time, Hank was only a teenager. It was then Hank told me exactly where my mother and I lived in San Francisco Chinatown, on Washington Street, right next to the Nam Yuen Restaurant, across from Portsmouth Square. And he added, "The building is still there."

I was overwhelmed, now at last I could see where I once lived.

Excited with all this new information, I asked Hank what my mother was like. He hesitated.

"Go on, tell me, I'm 63 years old now and it's about time I knew."

Reassured that I was serious, he said, "She had a temper, she was not very nice, and she was known for her 'not-all-there- personality'."

"What do you mean? Was she mentally sick?"

"No, no, she just wasn't there, that's all."

So maybe throughout my childhood my questions were never answered, possibly because they were too complicated and I was too young. They were protecting me, just like the Home, or maybe they didn't understand it either.

But I could grasp it now for I felt a deeper understanding of what my mother went through in her lifetime.

Questioning Hank for more information, I asked, "And how did she dress?"

"In San Francisco, when I saw your mother, she always had on a traditional Chinese dress with high heels. She was exceptionally pretty and when she powdered her face white (which was the fashion) and walked around Chinatown, she stood out. She wasn't like the other women; everyone noticed her." And Hank added, "Whenever I saw her, I was embarrassed."

"Embarrassed? But why?" I questioned. "Because we all thought she was a prostitute!"

My eyes widened and with a stunned expression I blurted out, "I thought so!" I kept my gaze on Hank and I could see he was relieved that I was not offended. So he continued almost apologetically, "After all, I was embarrassed because she had been my brother's wife and we didn't want anyone to know she was related to us."

I quickly called Ellen over to hear the story and said, "See, Ellen, he said so!" Ellen was immediately on guard and asked, "What did he say?" (for I had told Ellen a couple of times my thoughts about my mother being a prostitute and she had always said, "No.")

Hank once again retold the story. Ellen disagreed. Without hesitation she declared, "Oh you know how people talk, especially men. If a woman is pretty and not married, then she's a prostitute. And she concluded, "I never heard of that, it wasn't true."

I knew what Ellen meant, because I knew how people gossiped, especially in that era which had been so rampant with the prostitution trade.

But whether it was true or not about my mother, in the back of my mind there had been this thought (as a young adult), mainly because of the teacher's silence. Back then, if they had explained to me that my mother was sick, I would have been pacified. But given their secretive nature (my relatives included), I thought whatever happened or whatever she did must be really bad.

After the picnic, Jim drove Joe and I to San Francisco, Chinatown to the location Hank had mentioned. I stood in front and looked up at that tall white building and got goosebumps. I ran across the street (with my camera) to get a better view. It was unbelievable, this was the building where I had lived with my mother. It was as I remembered it. From the outside of the building I saw the opposite blank wall which had been my view. It was incredible, for even though I knew in my heart about the kitchen window with no view, it was good to hear from my uncle that I had remembered correctly.

Although I had been to San Francisco Chinatown many times, that day I saw things differently, for Chinatown was also part of my roots. This too, had been my beginnings with mother. I had come home. To think, I once walked hand-in-hand with my mother up and down those steep streets, passed crowded grocery stores, small restaurants and the old St. Mary's Church.

Back then, I spoke fluent Chinese with my mother, but I had lost that art. But I have never lost the memories of my mother. Those memories and the fact that she was probably from China was all I knew about my mother.

That Sunday was an unforgettable revelation and it was also very meaningful, for now I felt connected with my relatives.

Yet, there was still the lingering question of, "what was the emergency?" This age-old question now merge with Lorna Logan's remembrance of my name. Why did she remember my name?

Was it because my mother came to "920," seeking help when she was mentally ill? Or did she come to "920" seeking help for me? Could she have been one of the women rescued by Donaldina Cameron? And then there was the man dressed in white who visited my mother. Was he a boyfriend or what? Was he the cause of her downfall? Or like my father and me and other family members, was she also a victim of tuberculosis?

Also, why did my mother dress in somber black and resemble a grandma the day she left me at the Home? Was she playing a role and was this outfit reflecting her feelings of impending doom; for that day she knew she had to give up her last child.

I remember my mother's stonewall expression and I now know that deep within her soul, she was crying for help.

My poor mother, her entire family was gone. That day must have been a traumatizing day for her also.

All these and other questions will always be a mystery, but as one great man once said, "The greatest experience in life is the mystery." To a certain extent, I believe that's true.

Through my personal beliefs at this point in my life (different from my lessons instilled in us at the Home), I believe we pick our particular parents in order to learn different lessons in each lifetime. With this perspective I have come to terms with my chopstick childhood. My life has been good, maybe not like the old-fashion, traditional dream family, but I am at peace and I thank God that I am whole and well, especially in spirit. I thank God for the Occidental Board of National Missions for establishing the Ming Quong Home. I thank Donaldina Cameron for listening to her heart and I thank the teachers for caring and nurturing me when I was the most vulnerable. I especially thank the teachers for instilling in me a sense of pride of who I am and that I am proud to be a former Ming Quong girl.

And to my father, Mock Fun and to my mother, Lum Shee, I embrace both of you in love. I thank my sisters for being a part of my life. And for my brother, may the light of God surround you and keep you safe and whole.

And now, like a child who has mastered the art of using chopsticks, I am now filled. I am now satisfied. I hunger no more.

Thank you God. Thank you. Amen, amen.

Before Ming Quong

Even though the history of Ming Quong dates back to 1915, in reality it goes back further to the days of Donaldina Cameron (1869-1968).

As mentioned in the "Miss Chew" chapter, Donaldina Cameron rescued thousands of Chinese girls not only in Chinatown, but also in outlying areas.

As I told Ellen, "If Donaldina had known about your situation, she would have rescued you."

To me, Donaldina Cameron's story is similar to the good Samaritan story in the Bible. She was there to help, to aid, and to rescue, even at the expense of her own life.

To the grateful girls at "920," Donaldina Cameron was their "good Samaritan." Back then they affectionately called her "Lo Mo," the mother. And in Chinatown, she was known as the "mother of Chinatown."

But of course, by her enemies (of which there were many) she was known as "fahn quai," the white devil.

Also of great interest to me, was a former Ming Quong girl (before my time) who had been named Donaldina after Donaldina Cameron. In 1995 at Luella's 50th wedding anniversary, I actually saw her. It was an exhilarating moment, because this woman (whether she liked it or not) was an incredible link to the past. She was living history!

In 1994, the day I searched the files at "920," I was shown the infamous tunnel that once hid those terrified girls. Armed with my flashlight, I peered into the darkness and gasped. Even as an adult, who knew more or less what to expect, I was shocked. Under Donaldina Cameron's 43 years of service, "920" branched out to the Tooker Home in Oakland, then to the Ming Quong Home in Oakland adjacent to Mills College, and then a move to the site near Lake Merritt. The Ming Quong Home in Los Gatos was established in 1934. When I came to Ming Quong in 1935, the slave trade was coming to an end. The girls I grew up with were Chinese American orphans, and girls who needed care because of illness, unfit homes, abandonment, the death of a parent or because a parent had temporarily gone back to China.

And What Happened to the Girls?

In this brief synopsis of what happened when the girls went out into the world, I'm glad to say my "playmate," Carol was reunited with her mother. Carol had three children — two sons and a daughter. As an infant, a son was given up for adoption. The parallel in Carol's life was that when her son reached adulthood, he found her. At this unexpected joyous reunion, her son presented Carol with a bouquet of flowers.

Carol's lifetime of jobs up to the present has been waitressing at Chinese restaurants.

As for my "Tarzan friend," Beverly, when she got married, Carol, Paula and I were part of the wedding party. This was to be the biggest event, complete was a famous Hawaiian band for the reception. For Beverly's wedding day the three of us agreed that we would transform tomboy Beverly into a gorgeous bride. But when the day arrived, Carol's zipper on her formal broke, and we didn't get to doll Beverly up. But nevertheless everything worked out OK and Beverly looked radiant.

Beverly has two children. She became a CPA and then an attorney with her own successful law firm for 25 years.

As for my "generous friend," Amy, she retired as a secretary for the State of California in the Mental Health Department. She has two children.

A recent newlywed, she and her husband are world travelers. Their recent trip, their first to China, was a memorable experience, not only in terms of seeing China, but because

Amy met her 78-year-old sister for the first time. They had an interpreter with them as Amy's sister only speaks Chinese. The sister (now failing in health) has four grown children and grandchildren.

Multi-talented Rhoda once competed for the title of Mrs. California and was a finalist. She has two daughters. She retired after 40 years as an administrative coordinator from the Oakland Army Base. Rhoda, with her many hours of "kitchen work" at Ming Quong, has been teaching Chinese cuisine since the 70s. Currently she is involved with Martin Yan and Shirley Fong Torres' cooking schools. Rhoda also conducts walking tours in Oakland's Chinatown and has a business called Giftrends (gift baskets).

Our once-a-year visit to the Begonia Gardens. Nona, Amy, Bingo

And "Betty Boop," Bessie (Boots) with her same gentle demeanor has raised six children (five daughters and a son). Her oldest, Brenda Wong Aoki, is an award winning storyteller and performing artist. We used to vacation in Southern California and would stay at Boot's and Dave's home. They were our extended family. Their congenial family atmosphere was reminiscent of the popular television series, The Waltons. I used to call them the Chinese Waltons!

Bernice, "Bingo," was a well-known artist of the San Francisco Beat Generation. Her recent paintings are shown across the nation in special shows generally dealing with a social- political theme. Bernice has her own art studio and currently conducts art seminars with a Zen format in the Mendocino area. Other Ming Quong girls

265

have become nurses, doctors, office workers, social workers, teachers, college instructors and realtors. And many, now retired, are volunteer workers in their communities.

As for my life, I, like Bingo, had an interest in art. Frances Gok and I used to sketch endlessly while living at the Ming Quong Home in Oakland. Frances continued on with art classes at college, while I was self taught. Years later my charcoal portraits were displayed at the Kensington Library in Kensington.

My husband was a social worker and a teacher. We have one son.

For close to 49 years, I have owned and operated a clothing and gift store in Walnut Creek, significantly named Ming Quong. Adjacent to my store through a connecting archway is my son's jewelry and T-shirt store called, "MQ."

Running a store has expanded my horizons. It has taken me to unexpected places and I have done things I never thought I would have done because as you know, I am reserved! But because of my customer's various request, I found myself in several fashion shows modeling the store's clothing to raise funds for the Dean Lescher's Regional Center for the Arts in Walnut Creek. And on another occasion I spoke at St. Mary's college in Moraga about my childhood at the Los Gatos Ming Quong Home.

Speaking at the college redefined how I perceived my education in life. Because I had no interest in attending college, I knew that my life's experiences was my education. I also knew that everyone around me from all walks of life were my teachers whether it be an infant to a senior citizen.

So far the biggest, hardest and longest course in my education has been writing this book. In terms of years (5) I would say this is equal to a Master's and in terms of writing, equivalent to a Ph.D! And because I am my own teacher, I'll give myself a passing grade with room for improvement! With a note, to learn how to use a computer!

Through the store many customers have become friends. A special friendship with the renowned artist and jewelry maker Laurel Burch resulted in an earring name "Ming Quong for Nona" and at that time she deemed me, "The Radiant Light of Ming Quong!"

Today the Ming Quong girls still have a special closeness. There are a few girls I see frequently while others only at Ming Quong reunions (the last at Mills College in 1993).

Recently we celebrated Mrs. Lee's (now Mrs. Linn) 97th birthday (in 1997). Mrs. Linn's smile still radiates love and warmth; she is a wonderful role model. At this time the Ming Quong girls in attendance wrote a note to Miss Reber.

At our Ming Quong reunions, teachers have always been our honored guests.

Our reunions are always filled with an abundance of joy, but at the same time we are acutely aware and saddened that some girls will never join us. Because for them, the experience was not good and the others do not want the stigma of having once lived in an orphanage. These isolated few will not acknowledge former Ming Quong girls in public. But for the greater majority, our friendship will always radiate and whenever we see former Ming Quong girls, we feel instant camaraderie . . . it's like coming home.

NONA MOCK WYMAN

And What Happened to Ming Quong?

I'm glad to say that Ming Quong is still in existence. But before I begin about the Home, I should start at the beginning with what happened to 920.

In 1968, in honor of Donaldina Cameron, 920 was renamed the "Donaldina Cameron House," by March Fong Eu, who at that time was an Assemblywoman.

The Donaldina Cameron House has provided over 130 years of service to Chinatown. At present they address the problems of battered women and family violence and provide all-over counseling and tutoring for refugees and immigrants. They are involved in issues concerning housing for low income families. The Cameron House (as commonly called) conducts spiritual programs such as Bible studies and also provides recreational activities for the youth of Chinatown.

Cameron House is a non-profit agency of the Presbyterian Church, USA and a United Way agency.

The Ming Quong site adjacent to Mills College in Oakland was donated by Captain Stanley Dollar of the Dollar Steamship Lines. This choice lot close to a meandering creek was the first official facility named Ming Quong.

The building was designed by the renowned architect Julia Morgan. This architectural creation is reminiscent of Chinese homes one reads about in Pearl Buck fascinating books on China (I've read them all!).

The first time I entered this building (as an adult) I felt like I had been transported back in time to another world. In front, a wide winged open gate beckoned. Two large, royal blue foo dogs (used for protection) graced each side of the entrance. These porcelain foo dogs were gifts from Julia Morgan. Inside a large courtyard, flowers and lush greenery surrounded a fish pond, gold fishes reflecting the

268

Ellen's aunts, Sara & Yute at the Ming Quong home (adjacent to Mills College)

sun's rays swam amongst lotus blossoms and slender papyrus reeds.

Julia Morgan's creativity appears in unexpected places, such as closet doors. The time I stayed overnight my eyes were constantly drawn to the top of the closet where a small design in the shape of an old family crest had been carefully cut out (an ingenious way for circulation!).

That night, Mills had graciously invited us to stay after the Ming Quong reunion. This was an opportunity of a lifetime and I wanted to experience how it felt to be one of the girls who had once been privileged to live in this building.

That day I had been on the Ming Quong Reunion Committee and by the end of the day I was exhausted and ready to go home. But I'm glad I stayed. For that evening looking out my window with the view of the courtyard I imagined myself living there as a child and I knew I would have liked it.

But as an adult looking out that window that evening I saw the beautiful silhouette of the sloping tile roof against the moon's glow and I could almost believe I was in Shangri-La! What a treat.

This building with its rich history is definitely a place to visit.

Outside, eucalyptus trees line the pathway leading up to what is now Alderwood Hall, an alumnae residence faculty for Mills College. The name of this path is "Ming Quong Road."

Beverly, Loretta, Nona, Bernice Lee, Paula
Mills College reunion 1993

The Ming Quong Home near Lake Merritt was also impressive. It had the feeling of a grand mansion. Two foo-dogs also graced the entrance.

After this Home was closed, it was used by the American Indians for their Tribal Center. The building

270

was later demolished and is now the Merritt Bart Station.

Ming Quong – 51-9th St., Oakland, CA

The Ming Quong Home in Los Gatos (former Spreckles home) still exists and is today known as Eastfield Ming Quong (EMQ), a non-profit
agency which provides mental health services to emotionally troubled children and families of all races. Eastfield, a former orphanage in San Jose, merged with Ming Quong in 1987. Together this organization has served the community for more than 130 years and is Northern California's largest mental health resource for children and their families.

The Home has been remodeled several times over the years due to earthquakes and changes in use. Since my stay at the Home, a new street with homes has been added off to the side of the Home. Today this street is known as "Spreckles Way."

Presently there are 10 boys housed in a cottage on the premises. Another 25 children live in cottages at EMQ's Campbell facility. The organization also serves children through school-based day treatment, in-home and outpatient services, wrap-around services, 24-hour crisis intervention and substance abuse prevention education.

In 1995, a portion of the Los Gatos facility was renovated for use as a conference center to raise funds for

EMQ's programs and services. Local businesses and non-profit groups use the center for small meetings and trainings, knowing that they are contributing to the health and well being of some very special children.

EMQ also receives funding from the state, county, United Way, fundraising events like the popular Strawberry Festival, individual and corporate donations through the Children's Circle campaign (of which I am a member), and many support groups and hundreds of dedicated volunteers.

And today, I'm pleased to say that Ming Quong's old Chinese gate is still standing. This historic gate which once reached out to us in our time of need, continues to welcome children and families who are being served by Eastfield Ming Quong.

Old Ming Quong Gate. Ca, 1937

Thank You

It is done! I can't believe it. Now I can sit back, relax and thank each and every one of you wonderful people who helped and encouraged me in this endeavor.

First, heartfelt thanks to my husband, Joe, who encouraged the writing of this book and then with infinite patience listened to ideas and readings at all hours of the day and night.

Second, to my son Jim, for his valuable input and for allowing his employees, Leigh Carroll, Mary Stice, Meranda, Lee Ann and Joyce to help.

Third to Joe Fong, an Asian American lecturer, who insisted that this "rich history" be written! His critical advice helped set the background for my story.

And then my deepest appreciation to some very special friends who stood by me all the way, especially when I started to wane. These people gave so much of their time, each in their own way. Lissa Hallberg, Tanya Lonac, Cea Madrigal, Jody Offer, Trysh McGregor and Ash Mehta.

A grateful thank you to Ellen Ong, Les Ong, Hank, Awah, Judy, Betty, Ray Quan, and Rayni Ong.

And for my "Ming Quong family," Rhoda Wing, Bessie Aoki, Luella Mak, Beverly Chew, Amy Allbritten, Paula Wong, Bernice Bing, Emily Chow, Ethel Wong, Ruby Chow and Helen Kee for sharing their memories.

And to their families, Brenda Wong Aoki, Mark Izu, Dave Aoki, and Walter Ng.

Big indebtedness to Ben Fong Torres for

reading parts of the manuscript and for his frank comments.

Appreciation to Kayo and Lorraine Denham, Mabel Seid, Cindy Fong, Eta, Trumilla and Les Williams, and Kathleen Caldwell for their support.

A grateful thank you to new acquaintances Leonard Michaels of UC Berkeley who offered to read the manuscript and guide me in the right direction. And Nicolette Ha of San Francisco's China Books with an offer to list the book in their catalog. And for Ruthanne Lum McCunn and Beverly Lauderdale's suggestions.

Also friends at Eastfield Ming Quong, St. Mary's College and The Four Seasons Club (formerly the Chinese Women's Society); your interest is appreciated.

For all my wonderful customers at my Ming Quong store who found me immersed in writing or typing. Thank you for understanding.

Also, a separate thanks to some Ming Quong customers — Judith Sullivan, Ann and Alan Cohen, Jean Ortiz, Maureen Little, Roberta Wong, Dr. Janedare Winston, Dave Rogers, and Sue Trach.

Special acknowledgement to March Fong Eu, Jerry Doyle, Lucile Reber, Mrs. Linn, Charles Torrey, and John and Jean Chew.

And in memory of Karl Schwarz, a renewed friendship for just one hour. I thank him for the valuable lesson of living in the "now" and for reminding me that each moment is precious.

And finally, a big hug to my sweetest friend, Susannah Lonac. When we met I saw in her a reflection of myself when I came to Ming Quong; she was 2 1/2 years old!

Resources

Chinatown's Angry Angel (The story of Donaldina Cameron), Mildred Crowl Martin, Pacific Books, 1986.

Chinatown Quest, Carol Green Wilson, Stanford University Press, (the life adventure of Donaldina Cameron), 1931.

Chinatown Quest, Carol Green Wilson, (revised edition) (100 years of Donaldina Cameron House), 1974, Chinese Historical Society with Donaldina Cameron House.

Images of Long Ago, A century of people, places and progress (in the town of Los Gatos and the cities of Saratoga and Monte Sereno). Marbin Associates, 1987

Chinese Argonauts, Foothill Community College, Gloria Hom, 1971.

Asian Week, Ming Quong Home: helping girls for more than half a century, Gerrye Wong, 1991.

The Story of Chung Mei, Charles Sheperd, Judson Press, 1938.

A gift to Aafji, Marcus Bach, Sunburst Publishing, 1992.

Fifth Chinese Daughter, Jade Snow Wong,

Harper Brothers, 1950.

The Rice Room, Ben Fong-Torres, Hyperion, 1994.

San Francisco Chinatown, (a walking tour)
Shirley Fong- Torres, China Books, 1991.

The Dream Book, Betty Bethards, Inner Light
Foundation.

The Dream Dictionary, Isabel Woolever, Random
House 1970.

Chinese American, Stanford Lyman, Random
House 1974.

The Chinese of Oakland (unsung builders),
Eve Armentrout Ma, Jeong Huei, Oakland
History Research Committee, 1982.

The Great Cities, San Francisco: Time Life Books,
1979.

1000 Pieces of Gold, Ruthanne Lum McCunn,
Beacon Press, 1981.

The Chinese of America, Him Mark Lai, Joe
Huang, Don Wong
- Chinese Cultural Foundation, 1980.

Chinese Women of America, Judy Yung,
University of Washington Press, Seattle and
London, 1986.

125 years — Eastfield Ming Quong 1992.

Living in Ming Quong thesis; (a retrospective look at orphanage experience), Luella Mak, 1993.

San Francisco Chronicle, The Big Four, July, 1996.

San Jose Mercury News, Ming Quong bucked U.S. racism, Joanne Grant, 1-17-97.

Toward the Golden Mountain, (the history of the Chinese in the Santa Clara Valley), (An exhibit by the Cupertino Historical Society and Museum), John Handley, April, 1997.

Pictures from the Past

pictures from the past
breathing joy into one's soul
present moment blessed

Cover, 'childhood picture of author' (from Ethel V. Higgins personal album, gift of Jean Chew)

Ming Quong Home (Eastfield Ming Quong files, via Tanya Lonac)

The next collection of six pictures came from Charles Torrey, (the first caretaker at the Home). This happened because I gathered together Luella, Rhoda & Jean (also Ethel, but she came on the wrong day!) to volunteer our services at the Los Gatos Strawberry Festival. The Los Gatos Weekly ran a feature story about our "return" and Charles read the article and mused, "Is this the Nona Mock I once knew?"

When I arrived at the festival, there he was, "my dear old friend," reunited over 60 years later!

'San Jose Rose Garden,' 'Nona and older girls,' 'Girls on iron bars,' 'Outside the Rose Garden, ca 1937,' 'Old Ming Quong gate' (Charles Torrey collection)

'Twin goats,' 'Two teachers, Chew and Reber,' 'Three teachers, Davies, Reber and Chew' (gift of Lucile Reber)

The pictures from Karl Schwarz came about because one evening a group of his co-worker friends from Hewlett-Packard were reminiscing, when Karl asked, "Does anyone know a Nona Mock?"

His good friend, Art Fong and wife Mary piped up, "We do!"

By Coincidence, Mary is related to my now deceased brother-in-law (Ellen's husband). I used to visit the Fongs when I was in my teens. They lived a few houses away from the Mock residence in Palo Alto. They told me that Karl was very sick. I sent Karl a card and during his remission period he visited me at my store and surprised me with pictures from his childhood album. We had a wonderful, but brief time trading stories from our past.

A few months later, Karl unexpectedly passed away. A feeling of deep loneliness swept over me and in the silence of my soul I cried and thanked him once again for his presence.

'Los Gatos Elementary School Pictures and Signatures' (gift of Karl Schwarz, from his childhood album)

'Ellen's aunts' (from Sara Quan, gift of Ray Quan)

Other 'pictures from the past' are from my 'old Ming Quong album.' These photos were available for us at two Ming Quong reunions, by the head of the Home. Any fortunate girls who arrived early were surprised at these unexpected treasures from the past. Interested girls signed their names on the back of each picture desired. Throughout the years, some pictures were borrowed, traded or given to me.

In closing, I would like to share the story of what happened to Miss Higgins' pictures of Ming Quong. Miss Higgins bequeathed her personal photo album to one of her favorites, Jean Chew. This select album included the best pictures of the girls, some of which I had never seen. So, whenever Jean shared this album some girls would inevitably ask for their picture. Jean had mixed feelings about this, because she enjoyed the pictures and wanted to keep the album intact. So, this is what she would do; first, she would pause, look at the girl, then listen to her heart and then, with a warm smile she would relinquish the picture!

In foresight, Miss Higgins was so wise in passing on

this legacy to Jean.

As the saying goes, a picture is worth a thousand words or maybe two! And that conveys my deepest gratitude for all the above contributors.

Filling in the Blanks

Wendy (my designer) informed me that the second printing resulted in 6 blank pages! "Why?" I questioned. Wendy replied, "Because it's a signature." I then found out a signature is the way in which a book is laid out. So I learned something new!

Then to my surprise, Wendy asked if I wanted to write more! I blanked out! But not wanting to waste "pages," I conferred with Jim and Joe and here are some "fill-ins" which you would not know unless you visited my store or attended one of my book readings.

First, because I am a member of Eastfield Ming Quong Children's Circle, a portion of each book sold benefits this special group. When I send Eastfield Ming Quong a check, I have fun because I tell them "This is their royalty check!"

Second, should you be interested in booking me for a reading, please call or write me at MQ Press, 1517 ½ N. Main Street, Walnut Creek, CA 94596, (925) 939-8346, or e-mail me at NONA-MQ@webtv.net (thanks to Jim I now have e-mail!) About my reading-I'll be there, even if I have to close the store! I've done that a few times because I feel it is a privilege to be able to share the history of this great orphanage.

Also if any additional books are needed, please check with your favorite bookstore or call me.

Finally my deepest appreciation goes to "you," my reader. I thank you sincerely for your interest.

And now for my final sharing. One significant insight came my way when I spoke for the California Retired Teachers Association. This happened because of Reynold Lum, whom I met along with his wife at my store. At that time Reynold knew it was my birthday. So when he arrived for my reading, he surprised me with two beautiful long-stemmed roses, and yes, one was pink and one was red. He then handed me a birthday card, and inside was this moving haiku:

And a child asked,
"Is my mother still living?"
And someone answered, "Your mother lives in you."

Made in USA - North Chelmsford, MA
1288105_9780997748413
11.01.2021 1125